T0096683

CORN ETHANOL

WHO PAYS?
WHO BENEFITS?

HOOVER INSTITUTION

SHULTZ-STEPHENSON TASK FORCE ON
Energy Policy

The Hoover Institution gratefully acknowledges the following individuals for their significant support of this publication and the **Thomas and Barbara Stephenson Task Force on Energy Policy**

THOMAS AND BARBARA STEPHENSON

CORN ETHANOL

WHO PAYS?
WHO BENEFITS?

Ken G. Glozer
Former Deputy Associate Director,
White House Office of Management & Budget

HOOVER INSTITUTION PRESS
Stanford University   Stanford, California

The Hoover Institution on War, Revolution and Peace, founded at Stanford University in 1919 by Herbert Hoover, who went on to become the thirty-first president of the United States, is an interdisciplinary research center for advanced study on domestic and international affairs. The views expressed in its publications are entirely those of the authors and do not necessarily reflect the views of the staff, officers, or Board of Overseers of the Hoover Institution.

www.hoover.org

Hoover Institution Press Publication No. 569

Hoover Institution at Leland Stanford Junior University,

Stanford, California 94305–6010

Copyright © 2011 by the Board of Trustees of the
Leland Stanford Junior University

All rights reserved. No part of this publication may be reproduced, stored in a retrieval system, or transmitted in any form or by any means, electronic, mechanical, photocopying, recording, or otherwise, without written permission of the publisher and copyright holders.

A report prepared by the International Energy Agency is referred to in the Supporting Documents appendix to this book: IEA Response System for Oil Supply Emergencies, Copyright © OECD/IEA, 2010. (The complete report can be found at www.iea.org/ publications/free_new_Desc.asp?PUBS_ID=1912).

The following article is reprinted as Supporting Document B in this book: Doug Koplow, "Biofuels—At What Cost? Government Support for Ethanol and Biodiesel in the U.S.": Earth Track, Inc., October 2006, p. 17, available at www.globalsubsidies. org. Prepared for Global Subsidies Initiative, International Institute for Sustainable Development. It is republished with the permission of the International Institute for Sustainable Development (IISD).

The author would like to acknowledge the Environmental Working Group's website (www.ewg.org) as a valuable database resource on biofuels and farm subsidies.

First printing 2011
18 17 16 15 14 13 12 11   9 8 7 6 5 4 3 2 1

Manufactured in the United States of America

The paper used in this publication meets the minimum Requirements of the American National Standard for Information Sciences—Permanence of Paper for Printed Library Materials, ANSI/NISO Z39.481992. ∞

Cataloging-in-Publication Data is available from the Library of Congress.
ISBN 978-0-8179-4961-7 (cloth)
ISBN 978-0-8179-4963-1 (e-book)

*The author grew up in the coal fields
of Southwestern Pennsylvania in the 1950s.*

*He had the extraordinary good fortune to have
parents, MARGARET AND JOSEPH GLOZER, whose
life's goal was for their children to go to college, become
professionals, and not enter the coal mines to make a living.*

*Their foresight, dedication, and sacrifice made it possible
for the author to achieve their ambition. And the author is
forever grateful and dedicates this book to their memory.*

Contents

List of Figures

Preface

....

In recent years, the powerful U.S. economy has stumbled, and its economic core and wealth have diminished. It is therefore essential that American political leadership recognize the importance of designing and implementing cost-effective and environmentally sound policies and programs that complement and promote the market-based economy that has given Americans a high level of prosperity since the end of World War II. Competitive markets have served this nation well during this period, and competitive market policies should be supplanted only when more effective ones are found and proved.

But in the first decade of the twenty-first century, the George W. Bush administration, the Obama administration, and Congress have become enamored with a federal mandate, subsidy, and trade protection policy for corn ethanol. Federal energy subsidies for petroleum date back to the early 1900s, but as documented by two Department of Energy/Energy Information Administration reports, the rate of growth of federal energy subsidies spending is alarming.

Further, these massive and deep subsidies (grants, spending, tax credits, etc.) have been coupled with quantitative, fuel-specific mandates—the Renewal Fuels Standard (RFS) for gasoline—enacted in 2005, then doubled in 2007. This policy is a major federal-market intervention that seriously compromises and impairs a competitive market—much like the ill-fated federal-petroleum allocation and price controls of the 1970s first imposed by the Nixon administration and extended by Presidents Ford and Carter.

The RFS policy is not based on any objective empirical evidence that it works and that it is more effective than a competitive market policy in achieving either energy security or environmental goals.

It is therefore important to have access to the best, most objective information on whether this subsidies/mandate/trade protection policy works. The RFS has existed for more than three years, and there is now enough information to evaluate whether the policy in fact meets the claims made by its advocates. Part I of this book is a political history of federal ethanol policy. Part II contains the results of an evaluation of the claims the RFS policymakers made when Congress was considering the standard in 2005.

Acknowledgments

....

T he author is grateful to George Shultz, who served as secretary of three federal departments and now chairs the Hoover Institution's Thomas and Barbara Stephenson Task Force on Energy Policy, for the opportunity to write this book. His guidance and support were crucial to its completion.

John Cogan, Leonard and Shirley Ely Senior Fellow at Stanford University's Hoover Institution and Professor of Public Policy at Stanford, oversaw the research and preparation, reading many drafts and offering valuable insights, comments, and suggestions. In addition, the comments provided by a number of the other members of the Task Force on Energy Policy were especially helpful.

Richard Farmer, former senior economist at CBO, played a major role in shaping the content of the book and in completing Part I. His research, writing skills, and critical thinking added a great deal to the content.

The author is also indebted to Roger Williams who did an outstanding job editing the book and overcoming numerous software related technical hurdles.

The author also greatly appreciates the contributions of the many individuals and organizations that provided very useful information via interviews, published works, and information—including the Environmental Working Group, Department of Energy, Energy Information Administration, the Department of Agriculture, National Agricultural Statistical Service, and the Congressional Budget Office. While these organizations provided information used in the book, the views expressed herein are those of the author.

Political History

1

Introduction

This book has a twofold purpose. The first part is devoted to documenting the political history of federal ethanol policy and showing how it has evolved from 1977 through early 2009. Part I attempts to answer important questions about when the policy started, how it evolved, what the major political and market forces were that drove it, and, most importantly, which officials shaped it.

The second part of the book evaluates the major claims made by the policy's advocates over a thirty-year period. It assesses the following questions:

* Will the policy significantly reduce U.S. petroleum imports and increase energy security?

* Does using corn ethanol as a transportation fuel improve the environment?

* How sound are other frequent claims, including whether the policy reduces federal budget costs, reduces the U.S. balance of payments deficit, or increases rural employment?

+ Who pays for the policy, and who benefits from it?

All of that is important because the federal agencies involved (Environmental Protection Agency and the Departments of Energy and Agriculture—hereafter EPA, the DoE, and the DoA, respectively) have become promoters of the policy, along with such private advocacy groups as the Renewable Fuels Association, National Corn Growers Association, and Clean Fuels Association. They and others have made claims about the tremendous benefits bestowed on consumers and taxpayers in the process of securing enactment of the Energy Policy Act of 2005 and the Energy Independence and Security Act of 2007.

Those Acts contained the Renewable Fuels Standard, which requires petroleum refiners and importers to blend 15 billion gallons of ethanol annually in gasoline by 2015. That incentive supplements the tax credit of 45 cents per gallon of ethanol blended into gasoline and the import fee on ethanol imports of 54 cents per gallon. The latter two policies have existed since the early 1980s.

2
Ethanol as a Transportation Fuel: How Federal Corn-Ethanol Policy Evolved

Introduction

Ethanol, also called ethyl alcohol, is a pure form of alcohol that has been used as an automotive fuel since the first days of the automobile. Ethanol can be made by fermenting sugars (Brazil) or in the case of corn (U.S.), converting corn starch into sugar, then fermenting the sugars into ethanol. Ethanol can be made from other crops such as sorghum and other feed stocks, such as switchgrass, corn, and rice stalks. The latter process requires more processing steps and is referred to as cellulosic ethanol.

Ethanol is a high-octane fuel. Henry Ford championed it as an automotive fuel, and his Model T was designed to run on either pure ethanol or gasoline. Ethanol competed with gasoline in the 1920s and '30s in the United States, but eventually lost the battle as automotive-fuel consumption increased and major oil discoveries were made that provided the volume of fuel needed at very competitive prices. It reappeared briefly during the fuel shortages of World War II, but did not appear in consumer markets until the energy crises of the 1970s, prompted by incentives from state and federal governments. The incentives were aimed at growing the biomass, building the distilleries, and selling the final product, and to do that they made use of an extensive array of income supports, government research, tax breaks, loans, and outright mandates for use. Ethanol was not again produced in volume for automotive use until the 1970s.

Starting from a base of virtually no commercial sales in the mid-1970s, ethanol has grown to a point where it now accounts for over 6 percent (by volume) of U.S. gasoline sales. And current legislation mandates further increases that could take ethanol beyond 10 percent of sales by 2010. Today, virtually all ethanol comes from corn and sorghum in a distillation process that first isolates a sugar-rich byproduct from the production of corn syrup and animal feed, ferments the byproduct, and distills the pure alcohol from the fermented biomass. Distillation of ethanol for fuel is the same process used to produce alcohol for consumer beverages. Nowadays, almost all gasoline sold contains low concentrations of ethanol, but about 6 million vehicles (out of 230 million) on the road are capable of running on E85 gasohol—a blend of gasoline with up to 85 percent ethanol.

The first significant market for ethanol emerged mainly in the corn-growing states of the Midwest, where gasoline was blended with 10 percent ethanol to produce a fuel known as gasohol. The original rationale for federal support for ethanol was to help boost farm incomes, and that became linked to a desire to reduce dependence on crude oil imports. The many federal programs that support the industry acted to create a demand for the fuel, artificially lower its production costs, eliminate competition, and remove environmental regulations that restricted its production and use.

Three phases in the growth of the industry stand out. The first significant federal program to promote ethanol was the exemption—in 1978—of ethanol blends from a portion of the federal motor-fuel taxes. Combined with state tax exemptions, that made the fuel marginally competitive with gasoline in the Midwest and jump-started the market. Early federal programs to provide tariff protection against low-cost ethanol imports (produced from sugar cane in Latin America), financial incentives for ethanol plant investment and production, mandates for government purchases of alternative-fuel vehicles, and government research and developments spending also helped to develop the industry.

Then, in the 1990s, the rationale for ethanol support expanded to include clean air. For the first time, clean air legislation mandated the formulation of gasoline to create a new market for ethanol as an environmental blending agent—or oxygenate—to help reduce carbon monoxide emissions. Most of that oxygenates market was claimed by the compound MTBE (methyl tertiary butyl ether), which also helped to boost gasoline octane rating. However, when a growing number of state-level bans on MTBE use took effect, around 2000, the market for ethanol as a major octane enhancer began to increase.

Third, the most recent federal legislative action, in 2007, pushed ethanol as a panacea for global warming and U.S. energy security by mandating five-fold increases in the amount of fuel blended with gasoline, to 15 billion gallons annually by 2015. Those levels go well beyond limits for ethanol as an octane enhancer in a slowly growing gasoline market, and they could only be met if ethanol were marketed in concentrations well above the 10-percent level, perhaps going all the way to E85 gasohol in some regions.

Throughout that history, political activities of the groups representing corn producers and ethanol producers have been critical to the industry's development. The early advocates of the fuel adroitly used the national political process at key points to build a highly influential and effective lobby that today dominates the legislative process in Washington. In the early years, the lobby was dominated by the interests of the corn states, which were facing new competition abroad, excess production at home, and falling prices. Those corn interests included the newly emerging industry of corn syrup manufacturers (in particular, Archer Daniels Midland) with excess feedstock that could be made available for fermentation and alcohol production. All presidents have recognized the political importance of the farm states.

As a result, the DoE and DoA, as well as the EPA, have consistently supported the expansion of corn ethanol production.

The ethanol lobby had the backing of several groups, starting with policymakers who were looking at any and all technologies that could help protect the nation from oil-supply disruptions. Together those interests helped to secure the first federal-tax subsidy for ethanol and, by 1980, tariff protection as well. In 1988, the lobby added domestic automakers to the fold by crafting an arbitrary and generous CAFE (corporate average fuel economy) benefit for the production of "flexible-fuel" vehicles capable of burning E85 gasohol.

Early environmental support for ethanol had always been mixed. Advocates also pointed to the benefits of using it to lower vehicle emissions of carbon monoxide, and they worked to weaken government restrictions on gasoline vapor pressure—put in place to check other harmful emissions of ozone precursors and carcinogens—to boost the market for ethanol blending. But the growing concern with global warming in the past decade had the effect of pulling environmental interests strongly behind the most recent push to craft a strong renewable-fuels standard for the country.

Taken together, the power of such political concerns as energy security and a healthy environment, the critical placement of agricultural interests in federal politics, and the effectiveness of corn and ethanol lobbying have combined to produce several major—and many minor—political successes for ethanol. Among the most noteworthy policy developments of the past three decades are these:

+ Exemptions of ethanol sales from federal taxes on motor fuels and a tariff on imported ethanol, first authorized under the Carter administration;

+ Billions of dollars authorized for federal loans and loan guarantees for ethanol plant construction, greatly expanded in the Carter administration but mostly rescinded under Reagan;

+ Credits against fuel economy standards for automakers that produce vehicles capable of burning E85 gasohol (even if they seldom actually do), authorized during the Reagan administration;

+ Mandates for the use of ethanol (and other oxygenated fuels such as MTBE) in reformulated gasoline, authorized under the first Bush administration;

+ State-level bans on MTBE, starting under Clinton, which boosted demand for ethanol in reformulated gasoline and created a new market for ethanol as an octane enhancer;

+ Renewable fuels standards, authorized under the second Bush administration, that require annual quantities of ethanol to be blended into gasoline far in excess of octane needs—including 15 billion gallons of ethanol from corn and 21 billion gallons from cellulosic and other biomass sources.

But clouds have gathered on the horizon, as a world food shortage and record prices for grains emerge and some countries halt their corn ethanol program. Further, recent research has disclosed that corn-based ethanol may substantially increase greenhouse gas emissions, if indirect land-use impacts of forest or grassland conversions into cropland are properly taken into account. And even with ethanol prices rising sharply along with gasoline, corn prices rose even more quickly in 2008 (to over $6 a bushel in future's markets). That squeeze is greatly undermining the profitability of ethanol production. And in 2008 and 2009, the sharp, dramatic decline in oil and ethanol prices forced a number of ethanol producers into bankruptcy.

The following sections document the federal policy history of corn ethanol from the Carter administration through that of George W. Bush, describing the significant legislative and administrative building blocks and the evolution of today's ethanol policy. Included in this part are three important figures. Figure 2.1 displays crude oil prices year by year from 1970 through 2008, with each of the major federal ethanol policy interventions identified in the given year. Figure 2.2 displays U.S. corn production and prices year by year from 1970 through 2008, noting the years when weather had a major and adverse impact on corn production. Figure 2.3 displays year by year, from 1975 through 2008, annual U.S. petroleum imports and domestic ethanol production.

A. Carter Administration—Jump Starting a New Industry with Tax Incentives, Tariffs, and Financial Support

Summary

The decade of the 1970s saw sharply rising oil prices and outright shortages of gasoline supply, precipitated by the Arab oil embargo of 1973–74 (see Figure 2.1). Those problems were exacerbated by the federal system of crude-oil price controls and petroleum-product price and allocation controls, first imposed by the Nixon administration in 1971. Domestic events unrelated to the oil embargo also were disrupting markets for coal and natural gas. Subsequent reductions in world oil supplies, following the Iranian Revolution and related events in 1979 and 1980, combined with the partial controls over crude oil and gasoline prices still in

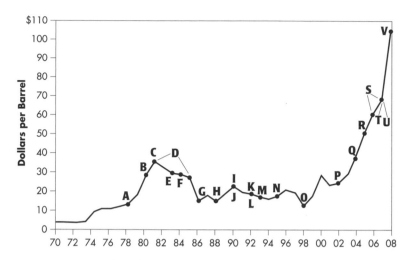

FIGURE 2.1   Crude Oil Prices 1970 to 2008

Source: Department of Energy (DoE)/Energy Information Administration (EIA).

Legend for Figure 2.1

A	1978	A 40-cent-per-gallon ethanol gasoline-tax exemption enacted.
B	1980	A 40-cent-per-gallon tariff on imported ethanol and a new federal loan-guarantee program for ethanol plant construction enacted.
C	1981	President Reagan abolished petroleum allocation and price controls, and established a competitive market-reliance policy for petroleum.
D	1981 to 1985	Phase-out of federal loan-guarantee assistance for ethanol plant construction.
E	1983	Ethanol gasoline tax exemption raised to 50 cents per gallon.
F	1984	Ethanol gasoline tax exemption raised to 60 cents per gallon and tariff on imported ethanol increased to 60 cents per gallon.
G	1986	Department of Agriculture (DoA) provided free corn to ethanol plant operators.
H	1988	Domestic auto manufacturers receive special Corporate Average Fuel Economy (CAFE) mileage credit of 6.7 times vehicle's actual Environmental Protection Agency (EPA)-mileage rating if vehicle capable of burning 85 percent ethanol/15 percent gasoline blend. Vehicles able to do that became known as FFVs (flexible-fuel vehicles).
I	1990	Clean Air Act Amendments enacted, requiring oxygenated gasoline in metropolitan areas not in compliance with the EPA's carbon-monoxide air standards.
J	1990	Omnibus Budget Reconciliation Act of 1990 reduced ethanol gasoline-tax exemption to 54 cents per gallon and extended it to 2000.

Legend for Figure 2.1 *(continued)*

K	1992	Energy Policy Act of 1992 included major ethanol subsidies: a $2,000 deduction for alternative-fuel vehicles, including FFVs; a $100,000 deduction for retail fueling stations that installed pumps for alternative fuels, including E85 ethanol.
L	1992	President Bush directed the EPA to change vapor pressure (RVP) to a higher level sought by ethanol advocates, even though doing so increased auto emissions and metropolitan-area pollution.
M	1993	President Clinton rescinded Bush's higher RVP regulation but required that 30 percent of the oxygenate blend be ethanol.
N	1995	The courts overturned Clinton's 1993 ethanol requirement.
O	1998	Ethanol gasoline tax-exemption phased back to 51 cents per gallon by 2005 and extended to 2007.
P	2002	Farm bill enacted, providing cash payments to ethanol producers.
Q	2004	Ethanol gasoline-tax exemption, whose cost was borne by the Highway Trust Fund, converted to a tax credit reducing U.S. Treasury General Fund Tax revenues.
R	2005	Energy Policy Act of 2005 established the Renewable Fuels Standard (RFS), mandating ethanol blending with gasoline of 7.5 billion gallons by 2012. Also, the oxygenate requirement for gasoline was eliminated.
S	2006/7	President Bush proposed his "20-by-10" energy plan calling for a reduction in U.S. petroleum consumption of 20 percent in 10 years. Two policies were proposed: one to increase light-vehicle mileage standards (CAFE); the second to require production of 35 billion gallons of renewable and alternative fuels (mainly ethanol) by 2022.
T	2007	Refiners sought liability protection for lawsuits over their use of methyl tertiary butyl ether (MTBE) blending in gasoline. Congress refused, triggering a rapid phase-out of MTBE and phase-in of ethanol—about the only blend that could now be used to enhance gasoline octane.
U	2007	Energy Independence and Security Act substantially increased the mandated use of quantities of the RFS that required 36 billion gallons of ethanol-blended gasoline by 2022: 15 billion gallons of corn based ethanol by 2014 and up to 21 billion gallons of mainly cellulosic ethanol by '22. 2007 Farm Bill reduced the ethanol tax credit to 45 cents per gallon and extended it to 2012; also extended the 54 cent per gallon tariff to January 1, 2009 and increased the tax credit for cellulosic ethanol to 1.01 per gallon.
V	2008	Texas governor files a waiver request with the EPA to cut the 9 billion gallon 2008 RFS-mandated quantity by 50 percent. He cited major adverse impacts, including increases in the prices of food and animal feed. In August, the EPA Administrator denied the waiver request.

place to further roil energy markets. Policy makers desperately sought new and reliable domestic supplies of energy—especially gasoline—and the advocates of corn ethanol took advantage of that situation.

Corn farmers and land owners, suffering from large corn inventories and low prices (a result of federal corn-price supports and related subsidy programs), were eager for new markets (see Figure 2.2). The rural communities supporting those farmers were equally eager for the economic development and jobs that would come with increased corn production and a new industrial base.

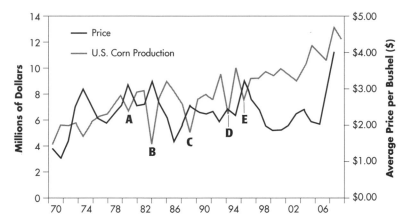

FIGURE 2.2 U.S. Corn Production and Prices

Source: DoA/National Agricultural Statistical Service (NASS)

Legend for Figure 2.2

A. Major drought; production declined 16.3 percent from previous year.
B. Major drought; production declined 49.3 percent from previous year.
C. Major drought; production declined 30.9 percent from previous year.
D. Major floods; production declined 33.1 percent from previous year.
E. Major drought; production declined 26.4 percent from previous year.

One firm, the Archer Daniels Midland (ADM), which enjoyed considerable political influence in Washington, served as the catalyst for enactment of many federal measures to promote the industry. ADM's political activities started with efforts to expand the market for high-fructose corn syrup (at the expense of domestic beet sugar and imported sugar); the activities included financial contributions to President Nixon that were revealed in the Watergate investigations.

President Carter campaigned on the promise to do something about the energy crisis. And in April 1977, just three months after his swearing in, Carter proposed his first National Energy Plan (NEP I). The cornerstone of the plan was a broad policy goal to "reduce demand through conservation." It included a number of specific targets for cutting the rate of growth of the demand for energy, substantially reducing oil imports and gasoline consumption, and increasing the production of coal and solar energy. The government support for meeting those targets was to come from an array of new taxes, regulations, and subsidies. In 1978, after much debate, Congress passed the National Energy Act—encompassing five different bills that implemented many, though not all, elements of NEP I.

But in November 1978, as the National Energy Act was being completed, the Iranian Revolution and strikes by oil field workers there precipitated the second oil-price shock of the decade. The Carter administration and the 96th Congress were again under extreme pressure to act on energy policy, and in May 1979, Carter sent Congress a second National Energy Plan. NEP II, continued the energy conservation strategy and most of the alternative-fuel supply initiatives contained in NEP I, including some that had not made it into the National Energy Act of 1978.

The 95th and 96th Congresses passed a number of key legislative initiatives to promote alcohol fuels. Although the initial NEP I plan had not included anything specific for ethanol, with the aid of corn interests, ideas soon came forward and, helped by commercial corn interests, made it into legislation. Additional proposals to promote the demand and supply of corn-based ethanol were specifically included in NEP II. Spearheaded by corn state legislators but supported by Members across the country, nearly 30 separate ethanol-related pieces of legislation (not counting appropriations bills) were introduced in the House and the Senate in the first half of Carter's term in office; more than 80 other bills were introduced in the second half. The new programs that were enacted ran the gamut of policy significance, from major tax-code revisions and manufacturer supports to minor public relations activities (such as the National Alcohol Fuels Commission).

Among the many initiatives helping to jump-start the industry in those years, three are especially noteworthy. The first of all ethanol policies, and among the most important ones thus far, exempted ethanol from a part of the federal motor-fuels tax. Congress added the exemption, not part of the NEP I, to the Energy Tax Act of 1978 (Public Law 95-618). (That measure was one of five components of the National Energy Act of 1978, the principal law implementing some of the Carter program.) The second involved an ethanol tariff of 40 cents a gallon, imposed in 1980, that covered nearly all imported ethanol; the tariff was among a number of "fixes" to the fuel tax exemption. The third initiative, also enacted in 1980, established federal support for the construction of ethanol manufacturing plants, through investment tax credits, loans, and loan guarantees administered by the DoE and DoA, and related measures.

A Fuel Tax Exemption: The First Major Boost to Ethanol Demand

The Energy Tax Act of 1978 exempted sales of gasoline containing at least 10 percent alcohol (by volume) from the 4-cent-a-gallon share of the federal tax on motor fuels that otherwise went into the federal Highway Trust Fund to pay for highway construction. At 10 percent concentrations, that exemption was equivalent to 40 cents for every gallon of fuel ethanol produced. The measure appealed primarily to the Midwest states, which added their own incentives to federal exemption, but it also had broad regional support in Congress. In the House, where all legislation on taxes must originate, bills containing a tax exemption provision had a combined 26 sponsors, including Representatives from states in the East, far West, and Southeast, as well as from the Midwest. Final passage of the Energy Tax Act came on a roll-call vote of 231 to 168 in the House (covering all five parts of the National Energy Act) and 60 to 17 in the Senate.

Both Democratic and Republican members of Congress strongly supported the ethanol measures of the Energy Tax Act, even though it was generally known that ethanol was far more expensive to produce than gasoline, was not compatible with the petroleum refining and distribution system, and caused problems with vehicle performance and emissions. The high cost of distilling ethanol from corn in part reflects the high energy requirements of corn farming, distillation, and transport to market.

Subsequent legislation proposed in NEP II to make the 4-cent exemption permanent did not pass, but in later years the exemption would be extended, expanded to cover lower concentrations of ethanol, and increased a number of times. A critical issue in all the subsequent debates was the Highway Trust Fund's loss of fuel tax revenues, which help to finance highway construction across the country.

An Import Tariff and Other Tax Measures to Help Domestic Ethanol Producers

In 1980, two additional pieces of legislation reinforced the retail tax exemption from the Energy Tax Act of 1978. One was the Omnibus Reconciliation Act of 1980 (Public Law 96-499), which established a tariff on imported ethanol equivalent to 40 cents a gallon. Consistent with the economic argument of protecting ethanol production as an "infant industry," the new tariff effectively ensured that all benefits of the fuel tax exemption went to domestic ethanol producers. Combined with high transport costs (especially all the way from receiving ports of entry to the markets of the Midwest, where most ethanol would be consumed for more than a decade), the tariff proved for many years an effective barrier to imports of low-cost, sugar-based ethanol from countries such as Brazil.

The other change to the fuel tax exemption was part of the Crude Oil Windfall Profit Tax Act of 1980 (Public Law 96-223). That act is best known for establishing a tax on the difference between market prices and controlled prices for different tiers of domestic crude oil. But it also created an income tax credit for alcohol fuel blenders, available as an alternative to claiming the exemption from the retail tax on motor fuels. Over the history of the exemption, most businesses would claim their refund on fuel sales, rather than against income.

The Windfall Profit Tax Act included a number of other measures designed to help ethanol producers. Among them: expanding a 10-percent investment tax credit on energy properties to include alcohol production and storage facilities; and establishing tax exemptions for municipal bonds used to finance alcohol production facilities. The act also streamlined the process for licensing distilleries that produce fuel alcohol (as opposed to alcoholic beverages).

Federal Loans and Loan Guarantees to Promote Ethanol Investment

The Crude Oil Windfall Profit Tax Act was primarily known for providing the funding source for a major federal program to finance the development of alternative-fuel projects. Together with the Energy Security Act of 1980 (Public Law 96-294), the windfall-profit measure made federal funding possible for a great number of ethanol investments. Ultimately, they proved to be of questionable merit, and the government wrote off large losses. At the outset, President Carter's Alcohol Fuels Program called for spending up to $4 billion in loans and loan guarantees for alcohol fuel and other biomass projects. That sum included $3 billion to be administered by the DoE and DoA and up to $1 billion from a new Synthetic Fuels Corporation

The Carter administration had first proposed a windfall-profit tax in NEP II. Broadly, the proposal was to establish a new tax on oil to fund the development of "synthetic" fuels—those derived from coal, oil shale, unconventional gas, and biomass, including ethanol—that could replace oil products on a large scale. As implemented by Congress, the Crude Oil Windfall Profit Tax Act authorized the funding program and the Energy Security Act, the spending program.

Specifically, the Energy Security Act of 1980 established a new federally owned business—the Energy Security Corporation, later renamed the Synthetic Fuels Corporation (SFC)—with the support of a proposed $88 billion in spending authority. Of that total, an initial amount of $19 billion was to be made available to pay for loans, price guarantees, and other assistance to private corporations for the construction and operation of synthetic fuels plants. The policy target for all those fuels was a total production of 1.75 million barrels a day of oil equivalent. Of the target, 1.10 million barrels a day (about 1.5 billion gallons a year, equivalent to 1.5 percent of gasoline supplies at the time) were to come from synthetic liquid and biomass fuels such as ethanol.[1]

But the program quickly fell on hard times. Congress appropriated only $19 billion for the SFC. The first "synfuel" demonstration projects selected for government funding quickly demonstrated major financial and environmental problems. And the ultimate sources of funding—windfall profits—dried up with the accelerated decontrol of oil prices and, finally, a collapse of world oil prices in 1981. President Reagan first reduced the amount of SFC funding and then eliminated the agency altogether, canceling its few major projects in 1986.

Other Energy Security Act of 1980 spending programs that would benefit ethanol have had a longer life. As part of its charter to support the production of alternative fuels, the act created a variety of alcohol subsidies and programs for ethanol research, education, and technical assistance. Most important, under the authority of Title 1 of the measure, Congress authorized $3 billion for synthetic fuels. The Congress subsequently appropriated roughly $1.5 billion to the DoE and DoA for loan subsidies–including loan guarantees and insured loans—for ethanol plants.

The guarantees were made available from both the DoE and Farmers Home Administration of the DoA. Insured loans for small producers were available only from the DoA. The goal of those lending programs was to achieve a level of ethanol production of 500 million gallons annually by the end of 1980. The act also provided for limited ethanol price supports in the form of federal purchase agreements—that is, guarantees that federal agencies would purchase at a fixed price some minimum amount from the subsidized plants.

In the passage of the Windfall Profit Tax Act, the nature of the political support for ethanol is difficult to discern from the voting record, because the ethanol provisions were not proposed or voted on separately from bill's basic crude-oil tax elements. The legislation was highly controversial. Floor votes in both the House and Senate returned it to committee. It was rejected outright in both chambers in multiple votes, and the Senate required four cloture votes before the bill could be brought up for a direct vote. The final tally on the total bill was 302 to 107 in the House and 66 to 31 in the Senate. It is likely that a coalition of farm-state Members was necessary to help offset the objections of oil state Members.

In contrast to the legislative battles over the Windfall Profit Tax, support for the Energy Security Act was relatively widespread. The Security Act was dominated by provisions that supported the creation of a synthetic fuels industry, and Members from all regions of the country appeared eager to pass at least one of a multitude of diverse project proposals for their jurisdictions. It is likely that that legislation would have passed even without farm-state support for the ethanol provision. Final votes were 317 to 93 in the House and 78 to 12 in the Senate.

An Emerging Ethanol Lobby: Establishing a Platform for Future Growth

In a very short period of time—from 1978 to 1980—the federal government implemented an ambitious ethanol program that set the stage for future growth. An array of federal subsidies and trade-protection measures were put in place to further this goal. There was overwhelming political support for ethanol within the Carter administration, with the National Corn Growers Association playing a key role in building it. The major and very influential advocate from the start had been Archer Daniels Midland, which quickly would come to be the largest producer of ethanol in the country. In addition, all of the Midwestern corn-growing states had trade groups representing their own local interests.

B. Reagan Administration: Greater Reliance on Energy Markets; Phase-out of Some Market-Intervention Policies

Summary

In 1980, after oil prices had more than doubled over the previous two years and with general inflation that year running at a near-record 9.4 percent, President Reagan campaigned on promises of a new direction in national energy policy.[2] Consistent with those commitments, his first Secretary of Energy, James Edwards, proceeded to implement a program of greater reliance on markets by "unburdening years of regulating market performance." That approach represented a major departure from the policies instituted after the first shock of rapid oil price increases in 1973 and 1974.[3] The new president believed that support for competitive energy markets would be the most effective policy to provide the U.S. economy with adequate supplies at reasonable prices.

Key proposals in the Reagan energy policy included: terminating the remaining federal petroleum allocation and price controls; abolishing the Department of Energy (and with the department, its vexing-to-conservatives regulatory functions); deregulating domestic natural gas prices; sharply

reducing the DoE research budget for solar and other renewable forms of energy; and phasing out the subsidies for
synfuels production, including those for alcohol fuels.

But implementing that Reagan plan would not be as easy
as proposing it. Corn and alcohol fuel producers had en-
countered major economic adversity during the period 1981
through 1989. And as they became increasingly organized
and politically active, they were able to hold on to and even
extend their beachhead at the federal level, despite the new
administration's emphasis on free markets.

The president made clear that he did not support subsidies or lending assistance for ethanol. For example, in 1982,
in response to a question, he indicated that corn ethanol
posed several problems: "The first being that it cannot be
produced at a cost that is competitive with gasoline itself. The
second issue is you actually use more energy than you get
back in ethanol. And if it can be economically produced, the
free enterprise system will see it happen." [4]

Industry supporters in Congress did secure enactment
of important provisions that would contribute to expansion of
the alcohol fuels industry by adroitly including those provisions
in major tax reforms and other measures the administration
wanted to see passed. But as oil prices declined in the early
to mid-1980s, the deeply subsidized alcohol producers were
not able to compete, and the small industry struggled to survive.

As a result of ethanol-industry lobbying and ethanol
support by key Republican Senators, the Reagan administration's attempts to reduce and eliminate federal subsidies
for alcohol fuel production achieved only mixed results. Two
major successes can be noted. One was the phase-down, and

ultimately phase-out, of the SFC in 1986; the other, a substantial weakening of the Carter plan for lending assistance by the DoE, DoA, and the Synthetic Fuels Corporation funding level from up to $4 billion to less than $400 million in actual loan-guarantee assistance provided.[5] A minor success came in 1982, when the Alcohol Fuels Commission—a small office that promoted the industry—was finally allowed to expire. (The commission first appeared as part of the DoE Reorganization Act of 1977, with a simple mission to report on the market and technological potential of alcohol fuels and then go out of business. But it had continued to operate and promote ethanol well past its originally authorized lifetime.)

Nonetheless, at the end of Reagan's second term, the tax-related alcohol subsidies and the tariff on imported ethanol remained in effect. Indeed, the exemption from the motor fuels tax and ethanol tariff were substantially increased under his aegis, from 40 to 60 cents a gallon.

Another action that had the effect of helping the ethanol industry, while running counter to Reagan's free-market principles, was the Alternative Motor Fuels Act of 1988. It provided a major although arbitrary incentive to automakers to build cars capable of running on E85 gasohol and other alternative fuels, at the cost of diminished fuel economy for vehicles burning gasoline. Vehicles that were capable of running on either gasoline or gasohol—flex-fuel vehicles, or FFVs—also received the CAFE credit. Car makers found they could produce FFVs for only slightly more than their gasoline counterparts and then receive substantial relief from the CAFE restrictions. According to the Energy Information Administration, there were in 2006 about six million FFVs on the road.[6] The direct benefit for ethanol suppliers, however, remained elusive. Of the nearly 162,000 retail outlets in the country in 2008, only about 1,600 offered E85, and two-thirds of those were located in just 10 Midwest states.[7]

Political Reality: The Emerging Ethanol Lobby and Growing Ethanol Production

Throughout the Reagan years, interests supporting ethanol became increasingly effective in Washington. The Renewable Fuels Association, Clean Fuels Coalition, and American Coalition for Ethanol all got their start in the 1980s. Those groups complemented the traditional grass-roots organization of the long-standing National Corn Growers Association and the newly established American Corn Growers Association. (The latter sprang from dissatisfaction over the reductions made in price supports for corn in the 1985 farm bill.) However, the influence of the dominant alcohol producer at that time, Archer Daniels Midland, probably was most significant in holding onto many of the gains from the Carter years and securing additional tax subsidies and other benefits.[8] Along with the farm groups, the ethanol lobby was able to turn on thousands of calls, telegrams, and letters to Members of Congress in support of the various pieces of legislation providing subsidies and benefits to alcohol fuel producers.

Key members of the Republican majority in the Senate strongly supported the tax subsidies for gasohol. Backers included Majority Leader Dole of Kansas, Percy of Illinois, Lugar of Indiana, Conrad of North Dakota, and Grassley of Iowa. Notable among Senate supporters outside the

Midwest was Pete Domenici of New Mexico, whose state included two national energy laboratories. That combination made it politically impossible for the Reagan administration to phase out the tax incentives for gasohol. Indeed, the opposite occurred: the White House accepted increases in the motor fuels tax exemption as a tradeoff for regional support for the highway bill and tax reforms proposed by Reagan.

Contributing to that changing political landscape, ethanol production grew tenfold in the Reagan years (see Figure 3). But the industry was very dependent on government, and even with its support, much of the early federal investment in ethanol production capacity was wasted. In 1980, most of the nation's fuel ethanol was produced by only ten plants. By 1984, the number of plants had grown to a then-peak of 163 commercial plants.[9] Many of them were very small, however, so small that they were idled almost as soon as they opened their doors.

As a result, by the end of 1985, only seventy-four of those plants remained, producing 595 million gallons a year. The high failure rate of the plants was caused not only by rapidly declining world oil prices, but also by the poor business judgment of plant owners that led to inefficiently small plant size and faulty plant engineering. Even with the very deep federal-tax subsidies and for some, loan assistance, they could not compete with petroleum-based gasoline.

Terminating the SFC and Rolling Back Ethanol Plant Loans

Consistent with their view of allowing the marketplace to determine production levels, the new Reagan administration

moved quickly to scrap President Carter's targets of producing 500 million gallons of fuel alcohol by 1981 and 2 billion
gallons by 1985.[10] In general, the Reagan plan for renewable
energy resources had little room for loans, loan guarantees,
and gasohol tax exemptions. Only the existing tax credit for
ethanol investment (20 percent) was considered worth keep-
ing.[11] The ethanol cause thus suffered the loss of the Synthetic Fuels Corporation (in 1986) and substantial cutbacks
to the loans and loan guarantees for alcohol fuel plants that
had been approved under President Carter.

During the early 1980s, the Reagan administration
struggled with how to dispose of the SFC. Its role conflicted
with the White House policy of market reliance but nonetheless enjoyed broad bipartisan support. Phasing out the
agency was therefore a major achievement of the administration, particularly in view of the strong opposition from the
most adamant synfuel advocates, Senators Domenici and
James McClure, who had played a major role in the SFC authorizing legislation.[12]

In 1980, Congress had appropriated $19 billion for use
by the SFC to subsidize synthetic fuel projects, with up to
a billion dollars available for alcohol fuels projects. In May
1984, the Reagan administration proposed legislation that
would rescind $9.5 billion of the $19 billion, with the remainder to be used on projects that the White House considered financially sound and sensibly scaled.[13] But the corporation never got around to making any awards for alcohol
fuel plants. The Consolidated Omnibus Budget Reconciliation Act of 1985 (P.L. 99-272) authorized the president to
terminate the SFC in 1986.

The second major achievement was rolling back a big part of the financial assistance available to ethanol producers through DoE and DoA programs. In 1981, as part of the Reagan administration's proposed amendments to President Carter's FY 1981 budget, language was included to rescind all but $250 million of the more than $1.5 billion that budget contained in appropriation authority ($745 million DoE, $525 million DoA) for loans, loan guarantees, and other financial incentives for alcohol fuels, biomass, and urban waste. The administration opposed any further increase in loan assistance authority and instead proposed to rely on the private sector and the earlier 20-percent investment tax credit to promote private investment in such facilities. The proposal to rescind the authority was approved by Congress as part of the Supplemental Appropriations and Rescission Act of 1981 (P.L. 97-12).[14]

Those actions undoubtedly saved the government a lot of money, given the experience of the few loans that got through. Using remaining appropriation authority that was initiated by the Carter administration, both the DoE and DoA had moved ahead to approve loan assistance for construction of alcohol fuel plants. The loan guarantees totaled about $420 million.[15] The DoE program offered to guarantee up to 90 percent of a project's debt, for loans that could cover up to 90 percent of a project's cost. The department made seven conditional commitments but eventually entered into only three loan-guarantee agreements.[16] Of those, one survived after several restructurings, and the other two eventually defaulted. Most of the DoA guarantees provided by the Farmers Home Administration also defaulted.

Increased Tax Subsidies for Ethanol Sales

Reagan's other interactions with the ethanol industry would be somewhat at odds with his free-market principles. The exemption from the federal motor-fuels tax for ethanol-blended gasoline (along with the alternative, income tax credit for ethanol blenders) was raised in 1983 to the equivalent of 50 cents a gallon of ethanol, for up to 10-percent ethanol blends. In addition, an exemption of 9 cents a gallon was approved for the E85 blends that could be consumed by flex-fuel vehicles. That was done under the Surface Transportation Assistance Act (P.L. 97-424), a comprehensive highway bill that the president supported as necessary to build and maintain the nation's highway system. The act, which generally provided for an increase in the federal gasoline tax and made other changes in the highway program, passed by a vote of 54 to 33 in the Senate and 180 to 87 in the House.

Subsequently, Reagan's comprehensive tax-reform measure, the Deficit Reduction Act of 1984 (P.L. 99-184)—also known as the Tax Reform Act of 1984, increased the subsidy of the motor-fuels tax exemptions (and the ethanol blenders' credit) even more, to 60 cents a gallon of ethanol for up to 10-percent ethanol blends. The House voted 268 to 155 and the Senate 83 to 15 in favor of the overall bill. For both increases, the administration had to accept large increases in the gasoline tax exemption for gasohol in order to secure enactment of broader reforms. Congress was able to secure enactment of the gasohol exemption increase with strong support from Members of both parties, especially those representing Midwest state agricultural interests. Senator Dole, for example, was a major proponent of the increases.

In addition, the continuing concern that Brazil would export its far-lower-cost, sugar-based ethanol to the United States produced political pressure to raise the U.S. tariff on imported ethanol. The Carter administration, in 1980, established that tariff on most ethanol imports at 40 cents a gallon. It was increased to 60 cents in 1984 under the Deficit Reduction Act (P.L. 98–369).

The "Free Corn" Windfall for Ethanol Producers

For most of the 1980s, U.S. inventories of corn were very high, exceeding 10 billion bushels—a consequence of the DoA's corn-production subsidies, good weather, and the increasing productivity of corn farmers.[17] Corn prices early in the decade averaged a comfortable price (for farmers) of about $2.50 per bushel. But in 1986, with inventories at record levels and continued high production, the price fell to only $1.50.[18] In that year, too, world oil prices declined to $14 per barrel. Producers of corn-based ethanol were simply not competitive with gasoline in that situation, even with deep federal and state subsidies. In 1986, in an especially noteworthy departure from Reagan's free-market principles, the DoA announced a program of providing free corn to ethanol producers. From the records available for public viewing, Archer Daniels Midland, the largest producer, seems to have received $29 million in free corn that year—over 50 percent of the total $54 million available under the program.[19]

CAFE Incentives for Automakers

Also out of character for the Reagan era, and definitely not part of the president's energy policy, Congress in 1988 enacted the Alternative Motor Fuels Act (P.L. 100–494) to provide incentives for the manufacture of automobiles capable of consuming alternative fuels, including E85 gasohol. That measure arguably stands as one of the most effective—although not necessarily most efficient—energy related actions of those years, and is directly responsible for placing more than six million flex-fuel vehicles on the road today. These vehicles were given a mileage credit of 6.7 times their actual mileage rating. They cost very little in additional manufacturing to produce. Currently, only about 1,500 gas stations, of nearly 180,000 nationwide, offer E-85 blends. This FFV mileage credit allowed the domestic automobile manufacturers to sell a large number of pickup trucks and sport utility vehicles, which helped turn the automakers into staunch ethanol advocates in Washington.

The program allows automakers to give highly favorable treatment to FFV vehicles in calculating their corporate average fuel economy. (The Energy Policy and Conservation Act of 1975, P.L. 94–163, authorized the government to establish average fuel-economy standards for automobiles and light trucks, with the goal of doubling economy by gradually increasing the standards from 1978 to 1985.) The result of the FFV credits is that automakers can reduce the required mileage for their conventional vehicle fleet below the CAFE standard otherwise set for them—initially by up to 1.2 miles per gallon and currently by 0.9 MPG. As it turned out, the benefits of those incentives have principally helped the sale of flex-fuel vehicles capable of running on either gasohol or gasoline. Very few other alternative-fuel vehicles are sold under the program.

As evidence of the benefits for ethanol producers, all the major organizations promoting ethanol vehicles wrote to the Department of Transportation (DoT) in 2000 in support of extending the program.[20] Automakers also strongly supported it, even though they had little interest in advertising their vehicles' dual-fuel capabilities. (Possibly they feared consumer resistance to new technologies. Subsequent changes to the law in 2005 would require that they notify buyers of those capabilities in order to receive the CAFE credits.) Interestingly, the remarks made by President Reagan at the signing ceremony for the bill stressed that it would take advantage of "existing government programs and mechanisms" and "was not intended to create massive new bureaucracies or new taxpayer subsidies."[21]

C. Bush I Administration: Mandating Reformulated Gasoline and Oxygenates

Summary

In 1989, the world was changing rapidly, with the Soviet Union starting to crumble and the U.S. economy headed toward recession. The new president, George H. W. Bush, had campaigned on a platform of a "kinder and gentler" government, which some interpreted as a step back from the intense focus on free markets during the Reagan administration. President Bush started his term, for example, by pursuing reforms to the Clean Air Act and authorizing the Secretary of Energy to develop a new National Energy Strategy.

However, much of the legislative agenda in his presidency would be constrained by the Reagan legacy of high budgetary deficits, which Bush and Congress addressed with new taxes and strict new budgetary rules to limit future increases in spending.[22] His presidency was also deeply affected by political developments in the Middle East. Energy policy stepped to center stage when, in August 2, 1990, Saddam Hussein invaded Kuwait, taking control of that country and its oil fields. World oil prices nearly doubled before the United States and a broad international alliance invaded Kuwait and destroyed the Iraqi army, starting with an air attack in January 1991.

Shortly before the allied invasion of Kuwait, Bush announced his National Energy Strategy and set forth his policy objectives: balancing our increasing need for energy with the need for reasonable prices; a commitment to a safer and healthier environment; a determination to maintain an economy second to none; and reducing our dependence on potentially unreliable suppliers.[23]

Ethanol would figure prominently in the new energy and environmental policies. Starting in the late 1980s, political concerns related to protecting air and water quality arose to join the issues of the previous two decades—promoting energy security and boosting farm incomes—in helping advocates garner federal support for ethanol production and consumption. Those years proved expansive for the ethanol industry. Senior officials of the Departments of Energy and Agriculture, as well as the EPA and the White House, were particularly supportive of ethanol policies. The decade would see major groups—relatively new to the cause—joining the growing ethanol lobby: the Governor's Ethanol Coalition, National Ethanol Vehicle Coalition, Ethanol Producers & Consumers, Renewable Fuels Association, Clean Fuels Coalition, Congressional Alcohol Fuels Caucus, and others.

The new policies with the greatest impact proved to be those that mandated the use of ethanol as a gasoline additive to promote cleaner burning. Although ethanol would not be the only product available to meet the new requirements of clean air legislation, the potential existed for ethanol to supply up to 2 percent of the gasoline consumed in major urban markets. In contrast, financial incentives never succeeded in expanding the ethanol market outside the Midwest, where supply costs were lowest and the states had developed their own incentives to complement the federal program. At that time, federal investment and operating incentives were largely redundant—or worse, given the existing fuel tax incentives and environmental mandates for ethanol use. Nevertheless, many deeply subsidized ethanol plants never proved economical.

Under the presidency of George H. W. Bush, one piece of legislation and several administrative decisions played the key roles in taking ethanol support to a higher level. First and foremost was the 1990 Clean Air Act Amendments (CAAA). The amendments specifically addressed vehicle-emission problems related to the formation of smog (ground-level ozone) and releases of carcinogenic chemicals from cars and trucks. The legislation mandated blending components of gasoline (which compounds must be included, which must be must excluded) and the degree of allowable tailpipe and refueling emissions. In addition, it challenged the states to set individual plans to comply with air-quality standards that would further affect the types of fuels and vehicles sold locally.

Energy policy followed environmental policy in the Bush I years. The president's National Energy Strategy, which included an important role for ethanol, was issued after the CAAA were enacted. And the most important legislation to result from that strategy, the Energy Policy Act, would not be passed until 1992, near the end of his only term in office.

Altogether, policy initiatives of the early 1990s changed the potential role for ethanol from that of a substitute for conventional gasoline to that of a critical gasoline additive. As a substitute, ethanol could only grow as the use of petroleum-based gasoline shrank. But as an additive, the futures of the two fuels were linked positively. However, two final hurdles remained before ethanol could secure a major niche in the national fuels market. One, the environmental benefits of ethanol blending from reduced tailpipe emissions of carbon monoxide were at odds with the environmental damage from increased evaporative emissions of ozone components and several known carcinogens. Two, ethanol was not the lowest-cost additive available to petroleum refiners for meeting clean air standards. That distinction belonged to methanol-based MTBE. The conflict over those issues—vapor pressure and MTBE—involved the ethanol lobby, the oil lobby, and environmental interests, and its resolution would await successive administrations.

The Clean Air Act Amendments— from Gasoline Replacement to Gasoline

In the debate leading up to the CAAA, ethanol supporters pointed out that ethanol could help reduce tailpipe emissions of carbon monoxide (CO). It results from incomplete combustion, and ethanol (an "oxygenate," with a high oxygen content) can facilitate a more complete combustion that reduces vehicle emissions of CO. But ethanol blended in gasoline also can create performance problems resulting from its high vapor pressure. That can result in vapor locks (gas bubbles in the fuel line), especially at high altitudes or in warm weather, and spur increased evaporative emissions of other smog-creating components of gasoline. Vapor pressure was always a problem for ethanol. Even before the Carter years, ethanol supporters in Congress had unsuccessfully introduced legislation that would direct the EPA to exempt ethanol-blended gasoline from the vapor restrictions on gasoline, put in place by authority of the Clean Air Act.

Part of the solution to the dilemma of carbon monoxide and vapor pressure was to create for gasoline different markets fuels that would require different levels of oxygenates. The CAAA required a basic reformulation of all gasoline to reduce carcinogenic components. The reformulated gasoline included a base level of oxygenates and was to be sold in summer in the nine metropolitan areas with the worst ozone problems. And gasoline with higher levels of oxygenates was to be sold in winter in thirty-nine cities areas with carbon monoxide problems.

It was never very clear just how important the new oxygenate standards really were to clean air, even in the carbon-monoxide problem areas. New cars with improved fuel injection, electronic ignition, and advanced catalytic converters were coming to market at the same time. But it appears that the ethanol interests prevailed over the auto-makers and oil interests in pushing the new oxygenate requirements.

Although the oxygenate mandates on their own seemed to promise a bright future for ethanol, it turned out that the product still faced a problem: in the market, it was not the lowest-cost oxygenate that could satisfy the CAAA requirements. That honor went to methyl tertiary butyl ether. MTBE blending to enhance octane had been widespread ever since the 1970s, when suppliers were required to remove lead from gasoline. (Compared with ethanol, MTBE was cheaper to make, and it could be produced at the refinery and blended with gasoline there. Further, MTBE-blended fuel could be transported in existing pipelines at no additional cost. Ethanol, on the other hand, was produced in corn-growing regions, far from the nation's refinery centers. Without the construction of special pipelines dedicated to holding potentially corrosive ethanol, it could only be trucked or moved by rail at relatively high cost.) As a result of that competitive disadvantage, the demand for ethanol remained concentrated in the Midwest in the immediate years after enactment of the CAAA.

The National Energy Strategy

Beyond the Clean Air Act Amendments, George H. W. Bush's support for ethanol was not spelled out clearly until he unveiled his National Energy Strategy in 1991.[24] The strategy was an important part of his energy policy, and it was decidedly more market interventionist than Reagan's version. It was presented as a "balanced program of greater energy efficiency, use of alternative fuels, and the environmentally responsible development of all U.S. energy resources."[25] The strategy included initiatives designed to reduce projected U.S. oil imports by 1.3 million barrels per day by 2000 and 3.4 million barrels per day by 2010 (under baseline projections) as a way to increase energy security in dealing with the aftermath of the Persian Gulf War.[26] The reduction in projected imports would result largely from increased production of alternative fuels (compressed natural gas, electricity, alcohol from natural gas, biomass, and coal liquids). The Bush strategy also cited, for the first time as national policy, the importance of reducing greenhouse gases—a goal that ethanol advocates would embrace in coming years.

The Bush I administration believed that alternative fuels would become more cost competitive as flexible-fuel and dedicated alternative-fuel vehicles gradually eroded petroleum's dominant role in the transportation sector. The DoE spent over two years in formulating this National Energy Strategy, and it guided the preparation of a package of implementing legislation that the president transmitted to Congress in 1991. Congress acted on parts of the plan, most importantly the Energy Policy Act of 1992 (PL 102–486), which included significant sections of Bush's alternative-fuels initiative.

The specific ethanol package included support for: extending the motor-fuel tax exemption for ethanol blends;

accelerating R&D to help commercialize the production of advanced transportation fuels from biomass by 2000; developing new energy crops via accelerated DoE and DoA programs; and providing for additional incentives for private and government fleets to acquire alternative-fuel vehicles. The FY 1992 budget for R&D was increased by 34 percent, to a total of $227 million, for those and other programs in the National Energy Strategy.[27]

Even before the strategy was released, but consistent with it, the Omnibus Budget Reconciliation Act of 1990 (P.L. 101–508) had established a program to aid small ethanol producers. From the outset, many people, especially those in farming communities, believed that corn farmers themselves would be producing significant volumes of ethanol. But that was not happening. To help address that failing, the 1990 act created an income tax credit of 10 cents a gallon for the first 15 million gallons produced by firms with an annual capacity of less than 30 million gallons. (The Energy Policy Act of 2005 would later expand eligibility to plants with capacities of up to 60 million gallons.) As a result, about 28 percent of U.S. ethanol production today comes from farmer-owned facilities.[28] The 1990 act once again extended the ethanol exemption from the federal motor-fuels tax, this time to the year 2000.

However, the gains for the ethanol industry in 1990 were mixed. On the negative side, the Energy Policy Act helped to pay for those changes in the budget by reducing the tax exemption and the income tax credit for ethanol blenders to 5.4 cents a gallon. Also in 1990, two administrative changes were implemented to boost the use of a particular non-alcohol compound, ETBE, for blending in reformulated gasoline. (ETBE is based in part on ethanol, but is chemically closer to MTBE.) The IRS ruled that gasoline mixed with ETBE would be treated as an alcohol blend, qualifying for the income tax credit available to other gasohol suppliers. In addition, the EPA ruled that ETBE would qualify as an oxygenate for purposes of the Clean Air Act Amendments. Ethanol advocates feared that expanded ETBE use would come at the expense of ethanol because, as an oxygenate and an octane enhancer, it had market advantages similar to those of MTBE. In particular, it could be manufactured and blended with gasoline at the refinery. The ETBE blend market however never developed.

The Energy Policy Act and Additional Spending Incentives

The key legislation resulting from the Bush I National Energy Strategy was the Energy Policy Act of 1992 (P.L. 102–486), which established a national goal of alternative fuels providing 10 percent of U.S. motor-fuel consumption by 2000 and 30 percent by 2010. To support those targets, the act extended the retail tax exemption for gasohol to blends using less than 10 percent alcohol; it also created two new tax incentives to benefit ethanol consumers and producers. Buyers and retrofitters of alternative-fuel vehicles (including 85-percent alcohol blends) could write off part of their cost—up to $2,000 for cars and greater amounts for alcohol-fueled light and heavy trucks; retail outlets that invested in equipment to store and dispense alternative fuels, including alcohol blends, could write off up to $100,000. Further, the act established a goal of 75 percent of federal and state fleets of cars and light trucks comprised of alternative-fuel vehicles.

Supporters did not get everything they wanted in the 1992 act. One further tax benefit for ethanol producers was allowed to lapse. Under the Crude Oil Windfall Profit Tax of 1980, ethanol had been eligible for the production tax credit available to producers of a number of alternative fuels. But further extensions of the retail tax exemption would come a few years later. In 1998, the Transportation Equity Act for the 21st Century of 1998 (P.L. 105–178, sec. 9003) further extended the exemption to 2007.

The Reg-Neg Controversy: Bush Takes Sides on Volatility Waivers

The provisions of the Clean Air Act Amendments that effectively mandated a market for ethanol as a blending component would prove to be more significant in promoting the substance than the various financial incentives the industry had received in the Carter years. But despite large increases in ethanol blending, environmental factors and economics still held ethanol use in check. Many in the environmental community believed that the benefits of ethanol blending from reduced tailpipe emissions of carbon monoxide—stemming from the more complete combustion of ethanol-blended gasoline—were outweighed by the harm from increased evaporative emissions of ozone components. (Gasoline with ethanol evaporates more readily, releasing those harmful substances during refueling.) On the economic front, petroleum refiners still preferred MTBE over ethanol as the lowest-cost oxygenate available for meeting clean air standards. The issue became one of the most contentious of the Bush I administration.

From the start, implementation of the reformulated gasoline program from the CAAA was complicated by the controversy over ethanol vapor pressure. The amendments include specific restrictions on gasoline vapor pressure, for environmental reasons as well as vehicle performance. That restriction had the effect of limiting how much ethanol, a highly evaporative fuel, could be blended into gasoline. Under an agreement signed by all interested parties, they and the EPA negotiated the final regulations to interpret the law—including vapor pressures to which both ethanol producers and refiners agreed. The process was widely known as "reg neg."[29]

But ethanol producers did not believe that the final rulemaking granted them sufficient relief from vapor pressure restrictions on gasoline. They balked at the final settlement, taking the EPA to court—to the consternation of oil refiners. In the heat of the 1992 presidential campaign, President Bush entered the controversy and ordered the EPA to change the vapor pressure limit to a level that the ethanol producers wanted. The producers believed that such a change would improve the attractiveness of their additive relative to MTBE. However, final action on the EPA decision, as well as disposition of the MTBE issue, would have to await action by the next administration.

D. Clinton Administration: Few Major Initiatives but Continued Production Growth for Ethanol

Summary

The Clinton presidency focused initially on recovery of the U.S. economy, starting with a fiscal stimulus package transmitted to Congress in the first few months after inauguration and followed by other initiatives for national health-policy reform, free trade issues such as NAFTA, and welfare reform. Beginning in 1994, with the mid-term elections bringing a Republican takeover of the House, both the President and Congress focused substantially on federal budget-deficit reduction. National energy policies and plans were relegated to a low-priority status. One exception: a Clinton proposal for a British thermal unit (BTU) tax in 1993, which was rejected by the Senate after being passed by the House. From 1993 to 2001, world oil markets were relatively stable, with low to moderate crude-oil prices in the $20-per-barrel range and ample supplies. At the end of Clinton's second term, however, an electricity crisis struck the state of California, causing brownouts and sharp increases in electricity prices.

The production and use of ethanol as a motor fuel grew moderately during these years. The market for ethanol was developing primarily as a gasoline octane-enhancing component, blended with petroleum-based gasoline in relatively small concentrations (up to 10 percent) that could be used in all vehicles—in contrast to the greater concentrations and special equipment requirements for E85 gasohol. Ethanol output increased from about 1 billion gallons in 1992 to 1.7

billion by 2001, driven mainly by the environmental requirement for oxygenated gasoline (see Figure 2.3). The corn and ethanol interests began to realize that, although a tax subsidy supported increased ethanol production, the mandated use of ethanol provided assurance that demand would grow.

Under the Clinton presidency, the country saw few major federal initiatives related to ethanol. In general, the Department of Energy continued to support an alternative-fuels strategy that mostly had been authorized by earlier legislation. One reason for the lack of new initiatives may have been related to the new congressional emphasis on budgetary restraint and a lack of interest by the Republican leadership in new spending programs. The ill-fated proposal for a BTU-based tax on all energy sources may have convinced the new president to stay away from energy issues. For their parts, the DoE and EPA were very involved with cleanup efforts at the nation's weapons-production sites and Superfund sites,

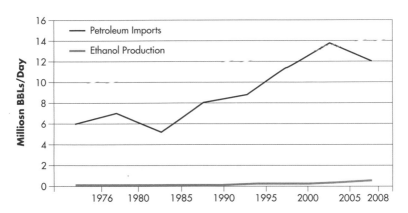

FIGURE 2.3 Annual U.S. Petroleum Imports Compared to Domestic Ethanol Production

Source: EIA, *Annual Energy Review 2007*: Table 5.3 Petroleum Imports, Table 10.3 Fuel Ethanol (adjusted for ethanol's lower BTU content)

as well as with other issues. In addition, the president and ethanol supporters were strongly rebuffed in his first year, when they tried to implement the Bush volatility waivers for ethanol.

State and court initiatives to restrict the use of MTBE for health and environmental reasons had a bigger impact than any federal actions on ethanol sales in the Clinton years. The concern was groundwater contamination from MTBE blended in gasoline and the adverse health effects of methanol—a major component of MTBE. Indeed, the elimination of MTBE was probably the most important action supporting the demand for ethanol since President Carter's fuel tax exemption. In the beginning, ethanol had not been the lowest-cost additive available to petroleum refiners for meeting the oxygenate requirements of the Clean Air Act Amendments. Refiners had preferred MTBE, which also was important for raising gasoline octane. But the attitude of refiners toward ethanol would change as a result of emerging local concerns about leaks of MTBE-blended gasoline from underground storage tanks and the associated contamination of ground water. A scientific link between the leakages and threats to human health was never fully established.[30] But state governments and the courts sided with local officials and activists against the oil industry and its supporters in Congress. With the encouragement of the ethanol lobby, state and ultimately federal legislators took steps to shut down the market for that lowest-cost alternative, and ethanol blending outside the Midwest took off. Most of the resulting increases in ethanol sales would be seen in the second Bush administration.

Settling the Reg-Neg Controversy with the Renewable Oxygenate Program

Although President George H. W. Bush overruled the EPA decision against the volatility waiver for ethanol, the task of writing that new regulation was left to President Clinton. His administration first acted to undermine the Bush ruling, then later wrote regulations that were even more support-ive of ethanol. The courts, however, set aside those stronger regulations.

The EPA under Clinton officially removed the Bush waiver in 1993, allowing the originally negotiated regulations for reformulated gasoline to stand. Under the original regs, ethanol supporters argued that the vapor-pressure specifica-tions precluded widespread ethanol use, although data on rapidly increasing ethanol sales seemed to undermine their case. Yet at the same time, in direct conflict with that ruling, the Clinton EPA appeared to side strongly with the ethanol supporters by proposing a Renewable Oxygenate Program.[31]

That program would have required that 30 percent of all oxygenates used in reformulated gasoline come from renew-able sources—in effect, from corn-based ethanol. A coalition of oil businesses and environmental groups strongly opposed the change. In response to a successful court challenge of the rule by two major trade associations for the oil industry, a federal appeals-court in 1995 set aside that ruling.[32] (In va-cating the proposed Renewable Oxygenate Program, the court held that the 30-percent ethanol mandate exceeded EPA's authority under the Clean Air Act, not that the EPA had violated the Reg-Neg agreement.)

Other Developments

Otherwise, successes for ethanol in the Clinton years were few and modest. In 1995, the EPA required that gasoline suppliers begin selling reformulated gasoline year-round (not just in the summer) in metropolitan areas with the most smog. But by that time, the major oil companies were already selling reformulated fuel in most markets, reflecting the economics of gasoline distribution.

And in 1998, in major legislation authorizing highway projects , the Intermodal Surface Transportation Efficiency Act of 1991, P.L. 102–240, Congress extended the ethanol tax exemption through 2007, but with a gradual scaleback to 51 cents a gallon by 2005. The exemption had been targeted for elimination by Chairman Bill Archer (Texas) of the House Committee on Ways and Means. However, Speaker Newt Gingrich (Georgia), reportedly at the urging of Midwest state representatives and ever-active Archer Daniels Midland, saved the measure.[33]

E. Bush II Administration: The Demise of MTBE and Enactment of the Renewable Fuels Standard Bring a Massive Increase in Corn Ethanol Production

Summary

In his first year in office, President George W. Bush faced two major events that would set the course for much of his time in office. They were the sharp downturn in economic

activity throughout that year and the aftermath of the terror-
ist attacks of September 11. The economic slowdown helped
prompt the President's call for widespread tax cuts in 2001
and provided an argument for increased federal spending
(and increasing budget deficits) in subsequent years. The ter-
rorists attacks—which presumably contributed to the economic woes as air travelers and consumers in general scaled
back spending—set the stage for subsequent U.S. military
action in Afghanistan and Iraq. And they set the stage for a
series of presidential energy-policy initiatives.

A relatively minor (in hindsight) third event in President
Bush's first year was the escalating electricity crisis in California. That crisis, disrupting power supplies at times to as
many as 1.5 million households and businesses in the state,
also played into the energy program the president would
propose.

In his second week in office, Bush established a National
Energy Policy Development Group. It was headed by Vice
President Cheney, included other cabinet members, and was
charged with developing a broad range of energy policies and
programs. As the president moved quickly in his first term
to develop a national energy strategy, his administration
regarded ethanol as one of the best means of achieving his
stated goal of reducing dependence of foreign oil.

In Bush's second term, persistently and sharply rising crude oil prices, gasoline shortages and sharply higher
prices following the damage from Hurricanes Katrina and
Rita, and political turmoil in such important oil nations as
Nigeria and Venezuela all combined to create a sense of ur-
gency that further supported the energy and ethanol agenda.

By then, the already well-organized and funded corn growers and ethanol producers and the extensive related lobby groups had forged new political alliances with environmental interests concerned about global warming: the National Corn Growers Association, Renewable Fuels Association, Governors Ethanol Coalition, Clean Fuels Coalition, American Corn Growers Association, National Ethanol Vehicle Coalition, Ethanol Across America, American Coalition for Ethanol, Nebraska Ethanol Board, and many, many others. A national mandate for ethanol production and other subsidies found widespread support in Congress. It also was advantageous that Congress in the Bush years was increasingly dominated by special interests and showed little budgetary discipline.

With a Republican president and, at the start, a Republican Congress, it is noteworthy that the specific actions taken to support ethanol production and use—mandating national quantities for gasoline blending, and supporting loans and other fiscal measures to aid producers—seemed to come full circle, returning to market-interventionist policies first developed in the Carter years. Also worth noting is that the end of the George W. Bush years would see the beginning of a breakup in the ethanol-environmental lobby. Environmentalists had come on board with shared concerns first about MTBE and then global warming, but the breakup started as the rapid increase of ethanol production led to sharply higher corn and other food prices, making more apparent the negative worldwide impact of ethanol policy successes on the environment and food prices. New research was showing that, compared to petroleum, gasoline corn ethanol increased rather than reduced greenhouse gas emissions. And food shortages and rioting in poor countries in 2008 stood created a very different situation than existed when 1970s corn surpluses first led American farmers to push for ethanol support.

The demise of MTBE was one of several important developments affecting ethanol output that occurred after the original tax exemptions, tariff protection, and fiscal support of the Carter administration. The substance's phase-out had started in the late Clinton years as individual states barred all sales of gasoline blended with the compound, and culminated with a federal ban passed in 2007.

Without competition from MTBE, the market for ethanol as an octane enhancer took off. But in the Energy Policy Act of 2005, lawmakers dropped the oxygenate requirement altogether and substituted a mandatory quantity of ethanol blended in gasoline. With the quantity mandate, the oxygenate mandate was unnecessary. (In return for supporting mandatory blend levels, refiners had sought legislative protection from lawsuits related to MTBE contamination of water supplies, but that the authority was not included in the final bill.).

Of greatest significance for the period during and after Bush II left office, and the greatest inducement to increased ethanol production in the history of the industry, is the enactment of the renewable fuels standards. In two legislative actions, those standards mandated large annual quantities of ethanol for blending with gasoline. The first was the Energy Policy Act of 2005, which would have required 7.5 billion gallons of ethanol a year by 2012. That program was succeeded by the Energy Security and Independence Act of

2007, which raised the annual standard to 15 billion gallons of corn ethanol by 2015 plus another 21 billion gallons in that year from hypothetical cellulosic sources. The 15 billion gallons would on its own represent a three-fold increase over the 2007 level and would threaten to push ethanol production to levels that might well prove not only unattainable but also undesirable. Such levels of ethanol use would require taking ethanol beyond its current role as an octane enhancer (generally in concentrations of 5 to 10 percent), where it can only grow with gasoline demand. Instead, it would be necessary to consume ethanol in the form of gasohol, in concentrations above 10 percent—even higher in some markets—with unknown consequences for vehicle maintenance and performance.

Vice President Cheney's Energy Policy Group

Vice President Cheney's Energy Policy Development Group recommended to the president more than 100 actions across a broad range of energy policies and programs covering electricity, domestic energy production, conservation, alternative fuels, and more; he accepted and began to implement most of them.[34] A significant number required congressional action, and in June 2001, the administration sent a comprehensive energy bill to Congress.[35]

The development group's report included these specific comments regarding ethanol: "ethanol vehicles offer tremendous potential if ethanol production can be expanded . . . [A] considerable enlargement of ethanol production and distribution capacity would be required to expand beyond their current base in the Midwest in order to increase use of ethanol-blended fuels." But the report made only one significant ethanol policy recommendation: to extend the fuel tax exemption for ethanol blended with gasoline. (The exemption was in fact extended but reduced to 51 cents a gallon in 2004, in the American Jobs Creation Act of 2004, P.L. 108–755.)

Congress debated and ultimately enacted two comprehensive energy bills during George W. Bush's second term, reflecting many of his positions but going well beyond the original call for a simple extension of the ethanol tax exemption. The development group's report and related legislation did not clearly establish a market-reliance policy, instead setting an agenda for energy that included a large number of federally sponsored initiatives. In basic terms, those federal demonstration projects and financial supports represented a return to the market-interventionist strategy employed during the Carter administration.

The 2002 Farm Bill: An Energy Title and New Ethanol Subsidies

As the congressional debate on comprehensive energy legislation continued, the agriculture committees of the House and Senate wasted little time in setting a new policy course that acknowledged the growing importance of fuel crops for corn- and soybean-growing regions and other forms of energy from biomass sources. The committees worked on a number of financial incentives to fund development projects and help support business investments, harkening back to the type of market intervention last seen on a large scale in the late 1970s.

The Farm Security and Rural Investment Act of 2002 (P.L. 107–171), which would govern federal farm programs for the next six years, was the first farm bill to contain an energy title that specifically authorized a number of energy production programs. It authorized federal procurement of bio-based products to help support the development of bio-refineries. It also authorized grants, loans, and loan guarantees for farmers and rural small businesses to develop renewable fuel projects. For fiscal year 2003, Congress appropriated $155.5 million for that program, and additional amounts were subsequently made available. In the farm bill, too, was a DoA Commodity Credit Corporation program to pay cash to ethanol producers for increasing their annual production of ethanol.

Because the energy title authorized renewable projects in general (not just those involving ethanol), political support for it was widespread in the agriculture committees. In 2003, the DoA approved 113 project applications, including wind and solar ventures, established in twenty-four far-flung states, as well those related to biofuels.[36]

This farm bill gave the agriculture committees a start on playing an increasingly important role in national energy policy. Congress would substantially expand that role in its next reauthorization of farm programs, in 2007.

Solving the Drain on Highway Trust Fund Revenues by the Gasohol Tax Exemption

Of less direct significance, Congress in 2004 resolved a long-standing political conflict arising from the retail tax exemption for alcohol fuels. The conflict pitted Members who served agricultural interests against those allied with transportation interests, such as roads and mass transit. Ever since the original Energy Tax Act of 1978 authorized the exemption, those revenues had been deducted from the portion of the total pot of motor fuels taxes that otherwise was going into the Highway Trust Fund. Transportation legislation in 2004 (the Safe, Accountable, Flexible, Efficient Transportation Equity Act, P.L. 109–59) directed that in the future the trust fund be compensated from general revenues, ending the ethanol-roads tradeoff.

Although that change didn't alter the pump price of gasohol and ethanol blends, it was important for the future politics of ethanol in Congress. In particular, the change may have contributed critical votes when Congress came to consider the biggest ethanol-support proposal ever, in the form of renewable fuels standards. For example, with ethanol consumption levels of over 3.5 billion gallons in 2004, a 51-cent fuel tax exemption could drain nearly $2 billion in annual revenues from road projects. To avoid major opposition from the highway lobby to new legislation that would greatly boost ethanol use, it was essential that general revenues— and not the Highway Trust Fund—be tapped to cover the lost tax dollars.

The Energy Policy Act of 2005: The First National Renewable Fuels Standard

At the end of June 2001, shortly after receiving the report of his Energy Policy Development Group, Bush sent to

Congress comprehensive energy proposals containing recommendations for legislative action to implement his National Energy Policy. The recommendations included expanding domestic energy supplies by encouraging renewable and alternative sources. Congress debated the various provisions for more than three years before finally passing the Energy Policy Act of 2005. During the period of debate, crude oil prices more than doubled—a fact that may have helped build the political pressure necessary for enactment. Most important for the ethanol industry, the 2005 act included a provision not originally recommended by the president, but one that would mandate for the first time the amount of ethanol that refineries, gasoline importers, and certain gasoline blenders must mix with gasoline in future years. The mandate was known as the Renewable Fuels Standard.

In its final form, the Energy Policy Act of 2005 mandated that 7.5 billion gallons of renewable fuels should be blended into gasoline annually by 2012. Under the statute, renewable fuels could include biodiesel made from soy oil or other cooking oils, natural gas produced from landfills, decaying matter, etc. But ethanol from corn was clearly to be the principal beneficiary. Along with the RFS, the measure repealed the oxygen requirement for reformulated gasoline, since it would now be redundant. Bush signed the bill in August 2005, and the EPA published a final rule implementing the standard in May 2007.[37]

Implementation of the standard was not straightforward, and in the future, it may prove difficult to enforce if it exceeds the amount of blending that refiners, importers, and blenders find profitable. For each of the suppliers of ethanol-blended gasoline identified in the legislation, the EPA determines the percent of ethanol that they must blend that year by dividing the congressionally mandated national quantity of ethanol for the year into the national gasoline consumption that is projected for the following year. The supplier then applies that percentage to his own gasoline sales volume to determine his minimum level of ethanol blending. State governors can request a waiver from the national mandate level of all or a percentage of the EPA-published blend percent, based on a claim of severe harm to the state's economy or environment or a claim of inadequate ethanol supplies. In addition, any person or company subject to the blending requirements can file for a waiver. But the EPA Administrator, in consultation with the Secretaries of Agriculture and Energy, determines whether the basis for the waiver is valid. In 2008, the State of Texas filed for such a 50, percent waiver, but the request was rejected by the Administrator.

The blending target for 2012 was more than double the 3.5 billion gallons of ethanol that refiners and other gasoline suppliers actually mixed into gasoline in 2004—nearly all of it from corn. And that 2004 level itself more than doubled that of 2000. As it turned out, however, the standard was relatively modest. Ethanol use was growing so rapidly with the demise of MTBE that the market would quickly outpace the act's scheduled increases. Ethanol supporters would return to Congress just two years later to lobby for much higher targets. That had the unintended effect of pushing not only the ethanol industry but also the food producers that use corn syrup and other products beyond their ability to supply at reasonable cost.

The proposal for a renewable fuels standard cleared the
Senate Environment and Public Works Committee and had
bi-partisan support in the Senate. Several versions of the
standard were considered over two Congresses, and numerous political coalitions formed and dissolved in the effort to
pass a very complex piece of legislation. The first response
of the House of Representatives to the president's energy
proposals was the comprehensive energy bill H.R. 4, which
was approved in August 2001; the 240-to-189 vote broke
largely along party lines in the Republican-controlled body.
Although that legislation did include some minor incentives
for alternative-fuel vehicles, it made no mention of a quantitative mandate for ethanol blend. The Senate, however, re-
sponded with energy bill S.1766, a measure that was sponsored by Senators Bingaman of New Mexico and Daschle of
South Dakota (both ethanol supporters) and that included
a requirement for blending 2.3 billion gallons of ethanol in
2004, increasing to 5 billion gallons by 2012. Congress, unable to reconcile the two bills in conference, postponed action until the following year.

Further attempts to pass comprehensive energy legislation were made in 2003 and 2004, but conference agreement
was rejected by the Senate. Another attempt to enact comprehensive legislation was made later in 2004. Finally, on a
vote of 244–178, the House passed the Energy Policy Act of
2004, sponsored by the Energy and Commerce Committee
Chairman, Joe Barton of Texas, which included an ethanol
mandate of 5 billion gallons by 2012. Barton's bill included
a safe-harbor provision to protect refiners who had sold
gasoline blended with MTBE from liability lawsuits; the

Senate bill, however, did not. It appeared that the oil state's support for ethanol was traded for some farm-state support for the liability waiver for petroleum refiners. However, Senate Energy and Natural Resources Committee Chairman Domenici, who had reintroduced his bill in the Senate, was unable to move a comprehensive energy measure in that chamber.

Not until 2005 were both halves of Congress finally able to agree on a renewable fuels standard for ethanol. Even then it took some trading to bring the House and Senate together. After the Senate had finally included a standard comparable to what the House had, a last effort was made to strip it out. First, the House passed the Energy Policy Act of 2005 (HR-6), a comprehensive bill that included a standard of 5 billion gallons by 2012, on a vote of 249 to 183. The Senate substituted and passed its version of the bill (S. 10), which included a mandate of 8 billion gallons by 2012 by a vote of 85 to 12. The Renewable Fuels Standard was controversial all along, and the opposition attempted to have the provision stricken from the Senate bill, losing by 69 to 28. After that last effort, the House and Senate conference on the bills quickly reached agreement and approved the report (74–26) the next day.

The American Petroleum Institute dropped its opposition to the RFS, reportedly in return for the provision to eliminate the oxygenate requirement. The National Petroleum Refiners Association continued to oppose the RFS. The final opposition, led by Senator Schumer of New York, garnered support mainly from Northeast and West Coast Members and a few fiscal conservatives. All Midwestern and other farm-state Senators voted in favor of the standard. The war in Iraq, rapidly increasing oil prices, and petroleum imports appeared to provide the impetus for favorable action. The Bush administration, in its Statement of Administration Policy, supported "increasing the use of clean, domestically produced renewable fuels, such as ethanol and biodiesel, and looked forward to working with Congress to ensure that a flexible, cost-effective renewable fuels standard is included in the final bill."[38]

The President's "Advanced Energy Initiative" and "the 20-by-10 Proposal"

As oil prices continued to increase above the 50-dollar-per-barrel level in 2006, the president announced in his State of the Union message an "Advanced Energy Initiative" that set a national goal of replacing 75 percent of U.S. imports from the Middle East by 2025 through advanced technology. The new initiative, the administration said, would achieve breakthroughs in technologies by increasing R&D funding by 22 percent. Coal, solar, wind, and advanced automobile technologies were all targeted. For the transportation sector, there would be advanced bio-refineries, more fuel-efficient vehicles, and the hydrogen fuel initiative. The goal for bio-refineries (a new word for ethanol distilleries that would process non-grain cellulosic material) was to "make cellulosic ethanol cost competitive with petroleum-based gasoline by 2012."[39]

In his State of the Union address one year later, Bush announced yet another program, this one aimed at reducing

U.S. petroleum consumption by 20 percent in ten years by substituting domestically produced alternative fuels for petroleum-based gasoline. That second, "20-by-10" proposal would be the basis for a new renewable fuels standard. Written into the Energy Independence and Security Act of 2007, it would increase ethanol production fivefold over the standard set in 2005—to 36 billion gallons of ethanol by 2022.

The 20-by-10 proposal included two initiatives. The first was to reform fuel-economy standards (CAFE) to make cars and light trucks more efficient by giving DoT authority to adjust the mileage standards rather than have Congress legislate tighter ones. The second was to increase the supply of alternative fuels by establishing a new standard that would require that 35 billion gallons of renewable and other alternative fuels be used annually by 2017. That was nearly five times the 7.5 billion gallon renewable-fuels standard approved just two years earlier, in the Energy Policy Act of 2005. In 2017, the latter would be substituted for 15 percent of projected annual gasoline use.[40] The proposal did not set quantities for each alternative fuel but opted instead for letting the market decide the quantity of each, as long as the mandatory quantity was met. In addition, the president proposed to double the size of the Strategic Petroleum Reserve, to 1.5 billion barrels.

Soon thereafter, the administration transmitted to Congress the Alternative Fuel Standard Act of 2007, which started congressional wheels turning on yet another major energy bill. In October 2006, to demonstrate his support for renewable fuels, Bush attended the Renewable Energy Conference—marking the first time any president had done so.

Debate over the new standards centered as much on concerns about greenhouse gases as on energy security, rising oil prices, farm support, and local air-quality issues. Environmental groups opposed parts of the president's proposed alternative-fuel standards because they included coal liquids and natural gas, neither of which are renewable. The manufacturing of coal liquids produced greenhouse-gas emissions that exceeded those generated by petroleum-based gasoline. Some of the environmental groups argued that there was now an extraordinary opportunity for corn ethanol, cellulosic ethanol, and biodiesel to meet the proposed massive increase in the standard. The traditional ethanol lobby was very supportive of those arguments.

Especially important for the debate were two recently completed major studies concluding that the United States had sufficient renewable-feed stocks to support large increases in the production of ethanol, both from corn and by means of as-yet-undeveloped technologies that would tap cellulosic and other non-grain sources. One study was by the Departments of Energy and Agriculture, the other by the University of Tennessee.[41]

The joint DoE-DoA undertaking, known as "the billion-ton study," was designed to answer the question, "Is enough biomass produced in the United States to make a significant impact on U.S. fuel consumption?"[42] That study focused only on estimating the existing volume of biomass material without addressing the range of issues that would have to be favorably resolved to gather the feedstock, prepared it for processing, then process the feedstock converting it into ethanol, then transporting the ethanol to retail markets for blending with gasoline then consumption. For fuel produced from biomass to be economically competitive with gasoline and technologically feasible, all the preceding steps would need to be accomplished and the end product ethanol would need to be economically competitive with petroleum gasoline. But the studies only covered the first step which was to complete an estimate of potential feedstock volumes. None of the other critical steps were address in any way. However, the results of the studies were broadly circulated, and biofuels advocates claimed they proved that the feedstock resources were available in 2005 for the large scale production of biofuels. Such claims are misleading.

The University of Tennessee followed with a 2006 study that outlined "how America's vast natural resources could be tapped to produce 25% of the nation's energy supply from renewable resources by 2025."[43] The findings of this "25-by-25" report were endorsed by over 100 major corporations and trade groups, and the document was widely circulated in Congress. The study assumed that the technology needed to produce cellulosic ethanol would be available and economically competitive by 2012, even though at the time only corn-based ethanol was marginally competitive with petroleum-based gasoline, and then only with large federal and state subsidies and mandates and at very high oil prices.

MTBE Phase-Out, Ethanol Phase-In

While debates continued over the first renewable fuels standards and subsequent 20-by-10 proposal for even greater ethanol mandates, another important change in regulation was rendering the mandates of the Clean Air Act Amendments and the Energy Policy Act of 2005 largely redundant. The change started at the local level, not in Congress or the White House, toward the end of the Clinton administration. The resulting boost to ethanol demand result more from emerging environmental concerns about the fuel additive MTBE than from any new-found benefits from ethanol. Those concerns arose almost by accident in California and elsewhere; officials in those locations discovered that when gasoline containing MTBE leaked from underground storage tanks, the MTBE contaminated the groundwater. MTBE was widely used by petroleum refineries (in preference to ethanol) to boost gasoline octane and meet federal oxygenate requirements for reformulated and oxygenated gasoline. With the groundwater discoveries, the debate over MTBE took on a life of its own, ignoring two facts: leaking tanks may have been a limited problem (and were, in any case, being addressed by earlier legislation on underground storage); and ethanol-blended gasoline would pose similar problems if leakage occurred.

As a result, several states brought litigation against the oil companies thought to be responsible for the leaks, with some states legislating bans on MTBE blending. First, in 1999, California announced its plan to phase out the substance by the end of 2003. Ultimately, sixteen other states followed the leader.[44] (Not surprisingly, nine of those states banning MTBE were in the Midwest and did not use it anyway.) In 2000, the EPA recommended that MTBE be phased out nationally.

Not until the Energy Independence and Security Act of 2007 did Congress finally require the substance's national phase-out. But a year before that, oil companies voluntarily ended their use of MTBE. (The Energy Policy Act of 2005 already removed the oxygenate requirement for reformulated gasoline, which undermined the companies' legal arguments that Congress had required them to use MTBE. And refiners had been unsuccessful in their efforts to gain legislative immunity from lawsuits arising from MTBE contamination.) With MTBE out of the picture as a low-cost octane enhancer, and with the oxygenate requirements of the CAAA still in place, the market for ethanol as a blending component of gasoline took off in a big way.

Energy Independence and Security Act of 2007: A Blueprint for Future Change?

The biggest boost to ethanol during the Bush II years came from the renewable fuels standard included in the Energy Independence and Security Act of 2007. If successful, the standard gives promise of taking the industry to even greater heights. But they may well be unattainable, and even just six months after passage, with international corn and food prices soaring, some in Congress appeared to be having second thoughts. As world oil prices declined in 2008 and early 2009, a number of ethanol producers became unprofitable and either shut down production or filed for bankruptcy.

The president's 20-by-10 proposal generated broad and intense debate. Both houses of Congress moved ahead with bills that differed substantially from what he originally proposed. In the end, he got much of what he wanted in the way of ethanol programs but none of those involving other alternative fuels, and ended up with initiatives he had not sought.

Of particular interest, the act included the first increase in fuel economy standards in thirty-three years—since the 1974 legislation that authorized CAFE. The corporate-average fuel economy of cars must now reach 35 miles per gallon by 2020, up from 27.5 MPG today. The act also dramatically increased the renewable fuel standard, to 36 billion gallons of ethanol by 2022 (including a small amount of biodiesel), with rigid annual quantities starting at 9 billion gallons in 2008 and increasing each year. Of that total, corn ethanol production is to reach 15 billion gallons by 2015 (double the 7.5 billion for 2012 in the Energy Policy Act of 2005), with the remaining 21 billion by 2022 to come from advanced, or cellulosic, ethanol.

The 2007 act does not specifically require corn ethanol, mandating renewable fuel blending. Instead, since the use of corn is currently the most cost-competitive method to produce ethanol, it is likely that the 15-billion-gallon portion of the mandate will be met with corn. Despite the president's request, nonrenewable alternative fuels—such as natural gas, hydrogen, and coal liquids—were not included in the standard. If the mandated quantities cannot be met, and if the heads of the DoE, DoA, and EPA agree—the act's administrative flexibility can be imposed in the interests of finding a lower number.

The path toward final legislation was relatively quick, if not direct. The House passed its first version of the bill in

January 2007, by a vote of 264 to 163. That bill included a fuel economy standard for light vehicles of 35 miles per gallon and a renewable fuels standard of 36 billion gallons of biofuel by 2022. The RFS included 15 billion gallons from corn ethanol by 2015 and 21 billion from cellulosic sources, plus a small amount from biomass biodiesel. The House bill also included a renewable portfolio standard (requiring that a specific percentage of all electricity generated in the U.S. be from renewable sources such as windmills, biomass or solar sources) for electricity generation, increased taxes on the oil and gas industry, increases in appliance-efficiency standards, and other means of reducing petroleum imports and greenhouse gas emissions

The Senate passed its version of the bill in June 2007, by a vote of 65 to 27. That bill included a 35-mile-per-gallon CAFE standard by 2020 and an RFS for 36 billion gallons of corn and cellulosic ethanol by 2022. It also included a provision to prevent gasoline price gouging and several other measures not acceptable to the administration. Bush's veto threats ultimately stripped from the bills in both chambers the provisions most objectionable to the administration, and Congress passed the revised measure. The final votes were 314 to 100 in the House and 86 to 8 in the Senate.

The political clout of the highly effective and broad-based network of companies, corn and soybean producers, trade groups, domestic auto producers, environmental organizations, and other political groups was amply demonstrated throughout the legislative process in getting passed and signed by the president what those very interested parties collectively wanted. Indeed, the process greatly resembled the proverbial snowball rolling down a long hill, getting larger and more potent as it goes.

Faced with rapidly rising gasoline prices and the sudden appearance of hybrid vehicles (without federal research support), the domestic auto producers and their key legislative allies, led by House Committee on Energy and Commerce Chairman John Dingell of Michigan, eased their long-term objections to CAFE legislation. In fact, the automakers joined with the ethanol lobby to support the RFS because it appears that the ability to sell flex-fuel vehicles may be critical to meeting the new CAFE standards at low cost. Recall that under the provisions of the Alternative Motor Fuels Act, flex-fuel vehicles receive favorable treatment in the company's calculation of its corporate-average fuel economy, enabling the firm to continue producing more cars with low fuel economy than would otherwise be possible. Indeed, automakers committed to build flex-fuel capability into 50 percent of all light vehicles produced in 2012 and thereafter. That special and arbitrary benefit had become even more valuable to the manufacturers under the 35-MPG standard. (In the first months of the Obama administration, new CAFE legislation would greatly accelerate the schedule for boosting fuel economy and make other changes in the CAFE program to close loopholes in the standards.)

Even though environmental groups had reservations about the local environmental impacts and greenhouse gas emissions of corn ethanol, most were keenly focused on global warming and the importance of supporting renewable forms of energy. They nonetheless secured a few, potentially important changes to the statute. One required that any new corn-ethanol plant not under construction at time of the bill's enactment demonstrate at least a 20 percent saving in greenhouse gas emissions associated with the plant's production. With recent scientific findings—reported after the act passed—pointing to unexpected emissions from the conversion of forest or grasslands to commercial use, the 20 percent standard could be difficult to meet. That is why corn-ethanol production facilities that existed or were under construction as of the date of enactment were exempted from this requirement. In addition, the greenhouse gas emissions savings for cellulosic ethanol over petroleum gasoline must be 60 percent.

2007 Farm Bill: Proposals for More Grants, Loans, and Other Subsidies

The 2007 farm bill, subjected to a presidential veto that Congress overrode, reauthorized federal agricultural programs and substantially expanded the range of assistance available to cellulosic ethanol producers.[45] New tax subsidies for ethanol were to be partially paid for with a reduction in the exemption of ethanol sales from the motor fuels tax, from 51 to 45 cents a gallon. Although the new assistance and tax provisions did not provide the direct basis for the president's veto, they did add to the cost of the bill, which was one of the primary reasons for the veto.

In addition to reauthorizing the ethanol-related programs from the 2002 farm bill, the new legislation included: billions for loan guarantees for investments in celluosic ethanol production facilities; a new subsidy of $45-a-ton for cellulosic feedstock production; and a production tax credit of $1.01 per gallon for cellulosic ethanol production.

The formidable farm lobby and ethanol interests were able to keep corn payments part of the new farm bill, even though corn prices were at record highs, rising in mid-2008 to over $7 a bushel on futures contracts and even though extending the ethanol exemption from motor fuels taxes of 45 cents a gallon would cost the government as much as $4 billion in lost revenues in 2008 and nearly $8 billion annually by 2015.

The final veto override vote in the House was a lopsided 317–109 and in the Senate was 80–14 overriding the Presidential veto by a wide margin.

The last year of the Bush II Administration focused on the implementation of the EISA. The corn ethanol industry's rapid capacity and production expansion from 2005 through early 2008 was halted by a sharp decline in petroleum and ethanol prices in the latter part of 2008. Corn prices also declined but not as much as petroleum thereby causing ethanol production to be uneconomic even with the federal subsidy. A number of ethanol producers stopped production and filed for bankruptcy. Thus, even with a federal tax subsidy, a mandate (RFS) and import protection lower petroleum prices have stymied the corn ethanol producers and reportedly are seeking even more assistance from the from the federal government.[46]

PART II

Evaluating Advocates' Policy Claims

3

Is U.S. Energy Security Strengthened?

Together with the alleged need to increase corn farmers' income, the oldest argument for current federal corn-ethanol policies has been the need to reduce the nation's reliance on imported oil and increase the security of its energy supplies. To date, that remains one of the benefits most cited in behalf of federal ethanol policies. (The other: ethanol reduces U.S. gasoline prices.)[1]

At a glance, the benefits from using ethanol to replace gasoline seem obvious. However, on closer inspection and with the experience of three decades, it is clear that current federal corn-ethanol policy does not now and will not in 2015 significantly reduce petroleum imports or increase energy security compared to a competitive market policy. The following analysis shows why.

Are U.S. Petroleum Imports Reduced?

In evaluating whether current federal ethanol policy reduces imports, a basic and important question must be answered:

how much ethanol would be produced and consumed if the federal policy did not exist? If petroleum-based gasoline were sold under competitive-market conditions—e.g., without mandated ethanol-blend quantities (under the Renewable Fuels Standard) or an ethanol tax subsidy or an import fee—how much ethanol would be produced and blended into gasoline? The answer is a substantial amount, because, under current EPA gasoline regulations, ethanol is the only octane-enhancing gasoline blend that refiners and importers can legally use to increase the octane rating of unleaded gasoline. For this important reason, refiners/importers would use a large quantity of ethanol.

In 2007, in response to a congressional request, the DoE's independent Energy Information Administration completed a comparison of a competitive-market policy to the then-proposed RFS mandate, tax subsidy, and import-fee protection federal ethanol policy. Forecasts were completed for each policy. Figure 3.1 compares the estimates for the EIA competitive-market policy versus the federal mandate, subsidy, and import-protection ethanol policy for selected years.[2]

As Figure 3.1 demonstrates, the reduction in U.S. petroleum imports on an annual basis, adjusting for the lower BTU content of ethanol compared to gasoline as estimated by the EIA, is not significant by 2015, when the corn ethanol mandate will be fully phased in. Further, a significant amount of petroleum will be consumed in planting and harvesting the corn and transporting the ethanol to retail markets. On a net basis therefore, U.S. petroleum imports are not reduced significantly.

(Estimates in billions of gallons per year)

	2008	2010	2015
Current federal ethanol policy	9.0	12.0	15.0
Competitive market (EIA estimate)	8.7	9.6	9.8
Increased ethanol—current policy	.3	2.4	5.2
Adjustment for ethanol's lower BTU content	.2	1.6	3.5
Total U.S. petroleum imports	176.4	180.6	191.9
Ethanol as a pctg of those imports	.1	.9	1.8

FIGURE 3.1 Ethanol Use Under Current Federal Corn Ethanol Policy Compared to a Competitive-Market Policy

Sources: Department of Energy (DoE)/EIA (Environmental Information Administration), 2008 "Annual Energy Outlook," June 2008; DoE/EIA, "Energy and Economic Impacts of Implementing a 25% Renewables Portfolio Standard and a Renewable Fuels Standard by 2025," Reference Case, Table 11, September 2007.

Under a competitive-market policy, according to the EIA analysis, ethanol imports from Brazil increase, as shown on Figure 3.2, compared to the results under current corn-ethanol policy.

Brazil is the world's lowest-cost high-production ethanol producer. The Brazilians' cost to produce ethanol is below that of the United States, because sugar cane is three times as efficient as corn at converting sunlight into sugar. Also, since Brazilian ethanol producers use the sugar-cane plant residue called bagasse (cellulose) as fuel for the conversion processing, very little fossil fuel gets used in the sugar cane-ethanol supply chain, which is similar to the cellulose ethanol process. And Brazilian sugar-cane ethanol has far lower GHG emissions than does U.S. corn ethanol.

	2008	2010	2015
Current federal ethanol policy	.7	1.1	1.6
Competitive market (EIA)	1.8	1.8	1.9
Difference	+1.1	+.7	+.3

FIGURE 3.2 Estimated Ethanol Imports from Brazil Under a Competitive Market Policy (billions of gallons)

Sources: Same as Figure 3.1

Up to 7 percent of U.S. annual ethanol consumption for fuel can enter the country tariff free via Caribbean nations. In addition, when world petroleum prices are high, imports could increase above that level: Brazilian producers could pay the tariff of 54 cents per gallon and still be profitable; that happened in 2008.[3] The difference between the competitive-market policy and current ethanol policy is about 1 billion additional gallons of ethanol from Brazil.

Brazilian imports would diversify U.S. supplies, because they come from another weather system, lessening vulnerability to Midwestern droughts and floods that substantially reduce corn production. In addition, Brazil is a democratic, market-based economy with a worldwide reputation for being a reliable supplier of ethanol as well as other major crops.

Increasing Energy Security?

Since current ethanol policy does not produce significantly lower petroleum imports compared to a competitive-market policy, the former does not increase U.S. energy security.

U.S. Vulnerability to Petroleum Imports

Ethanol advocates and others have argued that the United States is highly vulnerable to disruptions in petroleum supplies and the resulting sharp increases in petroleum prices. The facts do not support that assertion. Today and for the foreseeable future, the United States is less vulnerable to severe disruptions than is claimed for—the basic reasons and facts presented in the following paragraphs.[4]

In 2007, the U.S. imported 13.4 million barrels per day of crude oil (10 mb/d) and its products (3.4 mb/d). Of this amount, 2.6 mb/d was exported for a net import level of 10.8 mb/d. In 2007, that net import amounted to less than 30 percent of total U.S. energy supplies but 67 percent of total petroleum supplies.[5]

Figure 3.3 shows U.S. petroleum imports from the top fifteen countries. In addition to those, the U.S. imported petroleum from another thirty-seven countries, and is almost certainly the most diversified oil-importing nation. Import diversity and the fact that the vast majority of the imports come from outside the Persian Gulf reduce direct U.S. vulnerability to a physical cut-off of supplies.

Any major disruption to exports from the Persian Gulf would of course result in substantially higher world oil prices. But how likely is such a disruption? The answer is highly *un*likely. Contrary to some press reports and commentary opinion, the majority of U.S. petroleum imports are from friendly trading nations and allies. In 2007, only 2.2 mb/d came from the Persian Gulf (out of 17 mb/d exported

Source Country	2007	Source Country	2007
Canada	2,426	Virgin Islands (U.S.)	346
Mexico	1,533	UK	278
Saudi	1,489	Ecuador	203
Venezuela	1,362	Brazil	202
Nigeria	1,132	Kuwait	183
Algeria	670	Columbia	154
Angola	507	Norway	141
Russia	413		

FIGURE 3.3 2007 U.S. Petroleum Imports by Top Fifteen Countries (millions of barrels per day)

Source: DoE/EIA, "Annual Energy Outlook 2008," June 2008.

from the Persian Gulf). Further, there has never been a successful full or even partial closure of the Straits of Hormuz, the narrow body of water at the mouth of the gulf.[6] Even if Persian Gulf exports were interrupted for a few months, the U.S. would be unlikely to lose all of its imports. Therefore, statements about high vulnerability to events in the gulf are overstated.

Consider also the situation with several Middle Eastern countries, Nigeria, and Venezuela. All entail some vulnerability to temporary interruptions in supply. But each of the latter two countries has been a highly reliable supplier, and except for one or two others in the Middle East, exporting nations *need* oil-export revenues to meet pressing domestic needs.

Since petroleum is produced and traded on a world market, a severe interruption to supplies anywhere in the world has the potential to cause sharply higher prices that our country and others would pay even if we did not import any petroleum. To prepare for this highly unlikely but possible event, the United States and other major importing nations have implemented a number of measures, including maintaining a large quantity of strategic petroleum stocks. We have, for example, over 700 million barrels of crude oil in the Strategic Petroleum Reserve (SPR).

In addition, the US and 27 other countries are members of the International Energy Agency (IEA) under a treaty agreement. The IEA was established in 1974 after the first oil interruption and over the years has developed an extensive oil interruption emergency response plan and related measures. The measures include member country actions to build and hold petroleum stockpiles, demand restraint measures and many others in order to mitigate the adverse effects of a major oil interruption. Refer to Part III, Document A on page 163, and to the IEA's website for more detail at www.iea.org.

The United States gets 13 percent of its total daily petroleum consumption from the Persian Gulf, whereas other major importing nations—such as Europe, China, and Japan —depend far more on oil from that region.[7] Over the past thirty-seven years, there have been only four significant interruptions to world oil supplies, that is, four interruptions that resulted in at least a temporary world oil-price increase of more than 25 percent: the 1973–1974 Arab-Israeli war; the Iranian Revolution in 1978–1979; the Iran-Iraq war of 1980–1981; and the Gulf crises of 1990–1991.[8] The worst of these occurred in 1979 as a result of the Iranian revolution and resulted in a reduction in world oil supplies of about 3.7 million barrels per day for six months, or about 5 percent of world oil supplies (See Part III, document B, page 165, for a detailed Central Intelligence Agency history of supply interruptions to world oil markets since 1950.) The 1990–1991 event triggered a SPR sale, and oil prices dropped sharply immediately thereafter. The shortfalls from the 1970 including the 1979 interruption could have been easily offset from today's SPR if it had been available then.

The SPR in 2008 contained 706 million barrels of crude and 2 million barrels of heating oil, with a drawdown capability of 4 million barrels per day for the first 90 days. The estimated market value of this petroleum reserve, based on a $70-per-barrel crude oil price, is about $50 billion. Further, the International Energy Agency reports that IEA member countries hold some 4.1 billion barrels of stocks, of which about 1.5 billion barrels are government held or controlled, and that they have a drawdown capacity for six months averaging more than 6 million barrels per day.[9] Further, China is in the process of building a strategic petroleum reserve.

The bottom line is that the United States is well protected against any temporary severe interruption in world oil supplies. For ethanol to significantly improve this existing high level of insurance, the substance would have to displace substantial amounts of U.S. petroleum imports—on the order of several millions of barrels of oil equivalent per day. But it has already been shown that even at 15 billion gallons per year, corn ethanol does not reduce petroleum imports significantly. Thus, current federal corn-ethanol policy does not reduce U.S. petroleum vulnerability in any important way. In the most basic terms, there are not enough arable acres in the United States for corn production devoted to ethanol ever to reduce petroleum imports to a level that would improve energy security.

Any major U.S. effort to reduce petroleum imports would significantly impact friendly exporting nations. Since U.S. oil-import policy relies primarily on market forces, except for sanctions that prohibit petroleum imports from Iran, U.S. importers are free to select and contract with any exporting nation around the world based on price competitiveness.

Over 50 percent of U.S. petroleum imports come from Canada, Mexico, and Venezuela, all in close proximity to the United States. Those countries have always been reliable suppliers. Although the U.S.-Venezuelan relationship nowadays is contentious, the Venezuelan leadership understands that it would be very costly to cut off petroleum exports to the United States. Even if that happened, Venezuelan oil would go elsewhere, and U.S. imports would increase from other exporting countries. Further, Brazil has discovered billions of barrels—possibly as much as 35-40 billion—of new reserves off its coast, and in a few years is likely be a major exporting country. Also, Canada will continue to produce—and export across the border—crude oil from its tar sands.

For the other half of its imports, the United States can draw on widely diversified sources—more than fifty countries in all—and with the exception of those in the Persian Gulf, none poses a threat of a major interruption in supplies.[10] Even in the event of such an interruption, the United States and its allies have substantial reserve stocks and other measures available.

Those who promote uneconomic energy initiatives to reduce U.S. imports make another argument: high oil prices provide funds to certain oil-exporting nations that use the funds for things such as nuclear weapons. And these weapons, if developed or acquired, threaten the security of this country and its allies. If the U.S. does not purchase the oil, another country will. Further, an efficient, growing economy is critical and essential to the United States maintaining its defense forces and to ensure security. If the U.S. adopts a comprehensive and costly energy policy of substituting high-cost, uneconomical domestic energy (or conservation) for lower-cost imports, that will ultimately undermine our economic and national security. For example, if 4 million barrels a day of imports, at $75 per barrel, were displaced by a domestic energy supply costing $150 per barrel, the economy would incur an additional cost of about $110 billion annually. This excess cost would obviously reduce U.S. competitiveness.

The United States is already less than competitive in some world markets. If it imposes a further substantial economic burden on its economy by mandating, subsidizing, and trade-protecting uneconomic forms of energy, the result will be a further weakening of the economy and the nation's security. We are already running a trillion dollar-plus annual federal budget deficit, and adding the burden of uneconomic fuels will increase it by billions more.

Providing deep ethanol subsidies or imposing tariffs and mandates is not the most cost-effective policy for reducing U.S. petroleum imports. The United States has enormous oil and gas resources, offshore and onshore, that are economic to produce at current market prices. It is plausible, with current technology and in an environmentally sound manner, to increase domestic production substantially—thereby perhaps reducing imports by 25 percent over a 15-to-20-year period. This makes far more economic, energy, budget and environmental sense than does corn ethanol!

Are Domestic Corn-Ethanol Supplies Reliable?

Another important claim made by ethanol advocates is that because corn ethanol is domestically produced, it is reliable and not subject to interruptions. But are corn-derived ethanol supplies reliable year in and year out? The answer is no: weather conditions are very uncertain in the ten top-producing corn states, all clustered in the upper Midwest, which account for over four-fifths of all U.S. field-corn production. Droughts and floods often afflict that region. Historic evidence published by the DoA's National Agricultural Statistical Service supports the conclusion that corn-based ethanol will be far less reliable than imported petroleum because it is totally dependent on good crop-growing weather each and every year.[11] Since 1975 there have been a number of major adverse weather events in which U.S. corn production has declined at least 16 percent from the previous year. The events were either because of floods or droughts in the key corn-producing Midwestern states.[12]

Weather vagaries in the United States have a particular impact on *world* corn prices, because this country supplies about 70 percent of the corn traded on world markets, and over 80 percent of that is produced in just ten Midwestern states. Adverse weather-related corn-production developments in other major corn-exporting countries, such as Argentina and China, also are important. The uncertainties include long winters, delayed spring planting due to excessively wet fields, droughts, high temperatures during the growing season, crop pestilence and disease, and extreme weather that harms crop production or impedes planting, harvesting, and storage. And if predictions of global warming come true, the weather variations in coming years could become increasingly extreme.

The magnitude of weather-caused decreases in corn production is substantial, and it has a major impact on corn prices. Over time, corn production is simply not as reliable as petroleum imports. When, for example, has the United States ever lost 16 percent or more of its imported petroleum supplies for a year? That has occurred with corn production in each of the five years shown in Figure 3.4. It is not surprising, since major droughts and floods occur in this country about every six or seven years on average (although none has occurred in the past decade). Further, producer-held stocks are not likely to be adequate to meet demand at reasonable prices.

Year	Production	Percent Decline	Percent Price Increase	Cause
1980	6,639	−16.3	+23.4	Drought
1983	4,174	−49.3	+26.3	Drought
1988	4,929	−30.9	+30.9	Drought
1993	6,338	−33.1	+20.8	Floods
1995	7,400	−26.4	+43.4	Drought

FIGURE 3.4 Years that Floods and Droughts Adversely Impact U.S. Corn Production for 1975 through 2007 (in million of bushels)

Source: Department of Agriculture (DoA)/National Agricultural Statistical Service, "U.S. and All States Data-Corn Field, January 28, 2009."

If a 30 percent decline in corn production were to occur when the RFS fully phases in (2015), ethanol would claim over 40 percent of that year's entire corn crop. The nation would face a very difficult choice prioritizing food, fuel, and exports. Corn is an important food commodity, and if it is in extremely short supply, food prices will soar. That happened in 2008. Low-income groups suffer the most when this occurs.

Ethanol interests have claimed that new, drought-resistant seeds and improved cultivation practices will mitigate the impact of droughts. Although no major drought has occurred since 1995, logic argues that there will be another one. And flooding can be as damaging as drought: in 2008, major flooding in Iowa and surrounding states drove corn futures to nearly $8 per bushel. Some ethanol producers shut down or reduced plant throughput.[13]

A recently published report by the Environmental Working Group, entitled "Biofuels and Bad Weather," documents the major swings in U.S. corn production the elements have caused. EWG founder Ken Cook described the U.S. government's approach to the food supply as a "hope for good weather policy". Bad weather is inevitable, and so are the resulting losses in corn production.

A further weather-related threat is severe drought or flood in other major grain-producing regions of the world, causing sharp price increases. Prior to the ethanol mandate, U.S. producers had some flexibility to respond by increasing production, often through the use of carryover stocks. This flexibility is now far more limited, because all available arable acres will be committed to corn and corn stocks have been drawn down to record low levels. The end result will be an inability to respond to sharply higher prices.

Other Sources of Corn-Market Uncertainty Exist. Many other countries have their own crop-support programs, none of which are managed in coordination with the United States. And faced with any prospect of domestic shortage (whether real or brought on by price controls), every affected country could be expected to restrict its critical food exports in its own interest. That was the situation with rice exports from Asia in 2008. Despite an increased rice harvest that year, concerns about high food prices and the prospect of shortages prompted such countries as India to restrict the sales of the commodity to the rest of the world. That political, but natural, response exacerbated the price increase.

Beyond the risks associated with corn production lie additional uncertainties inherent in the production and distribution of ethanol. At a basic level, corn can be diverted to food uses, industrial uses, and animal feed. In the second category are the production of corn syrup and fuel ethanol. At the other end of the ethanol production process are by-products used for animal feed. Ethanol economics feel the effects of developments in all other markets, and uncertainties there will bring uncertainties in ethanol prices as well. In the spring of 2009, more than 2 billion gallons of capacity lay idle because of low gasoline prices and high corn prices, and a number of ethanol producers filed for bankruptcy. Even with a deep federal subsidy and import protection, corn ethanol production was at that point not economically feasible.

Distribution of ethanol to retail gasoline-distribution points may present a special vulnerability. The corn-growing region of the Midwest is remote from the large refining and gasoline-consuming centers on the East, Gulf, and West coasts. Not only must adequate supplies of ethanol be distilled each year, they also must move great distances at the right times of the year to be blended with gasoline for retail consumption. Bottlenecks in ethanol transportation were a particular problem in the spring of 2006, when petroleum refiners across a broad front halted their use of methyl tertiary butyl ether to enhance gasoline's octane content. Enough ethanol existed to replace that MTBE, but the industry experienced great difficulty in getting the ethanol to the West Coast and Gulf regions that needed it. Ethanol prices jumped sharply that year.

In sum, to the extent that ethanol displaces petroleum in the gasoline market, our gasoline supply will be less reliable than if it were entirely based on petroleum. The reasons are: recurring unreliable weather adversely affecting corn production; the nation's existing high level of protection against petroleum-supply interruptions; and the counterintuitive fact that there has never been an interruption of as much as 16 percent of world petroleum supplies lasting as long as a year. As mentioned earlier, the worst petroleum-supply interruption occurred in 1979, lasted six months, and reduced the world's oil supply an average of 3.7 million barrels per day—only about or roughly 5 percent.[14]

4

Does the Environment Benefit?

A nother major claim long made by advocates of the policy is that ethanol reduces greenhouse gas emissions by an average of 20 percent compared to petroleum gasoline and also reduces other vehicle tail-pipe emissions.

The decision-making that underlay the ethanol mandates of the Energy Policy Act of 2005 and the Energy Independence and Security Act of 2007 (EISA 2007) was not accompanied by a comprehensive assessment of the environmental impacts of the new renewable fuels standards. To assess those impacts, federal policy makers apparently simply assumed that ethanol would prove environmentally superior to petroleum gasoline, both globally and locally. Globally, the benefits were to come from reduced emissions of greenhouse gases, since corn is a renewable source of energy. Further gains at reduced costs were anticipated, too, as today's investments in corn ethanol paved the way for biofuels of the future. Locally, motor vehicles were supposed to run more cleanly on ethanol blends than on gasoline.

Reducing Greenhouse Gas Emissions

Perhaps the most critical argument swaying legislators as they enacted the new ethanol mandate in 2007 was a promise of reduced emissions of greenhouse gases (GHG). That promise rested on federal government claims of an average, compared with petroleum-based gasoline, of 20 percent savings in GHG emissions on a life-cycle basis (from production in the field to consumption on the road). The claim was based on an obscure, 1999 DoA study of the land-use impacts of a 4 billion-gallon RFS by 2010.[15] Since the 15 billion-gallon RFS enacted in 2007 is nearly four times that large, this fact alone should have prompted a new assessment.

Further, the findings of more-recent scientific research— including university studies at Princeton and the University of Minnesota—provide strong evidence that GHG emissions may actually increase when the analysis accounts for indirect changes in land use from replacing other crops and untilled land with corn. Yet through January 2009, the EPA still promoted and endorsed the 15- to 20-percent average GHG savings.[16]

Language in the 2007 EISA establishing the ethanol mandate of 15 billion gallons per year hinted at a lack of confidence in the scientific underpinnings of the claimed savings in greenhouse gas emissions. The EISA required that future corn-ethanol plants achieve a 20 percent reduction in emissions relative to gasoline. But at the same time, ethanol interests lobbied hard and successfully to exempt (or grandfather) all existing ethanol plants from any requirement to actually achieve those GHG reductions. The exemption included plants either planned or under construction as of the date of enactment. Specifically, the act provides the EPA Administrator with authority to waive the 20 percent GHG-savings requirement under certain conditions as long as an estimated savings of half that amount is achieved. But early indications from the EPA suggest that that provision will exempt (or grandfather) as much as 14 billion gallons per year of domestic corn-ethanol capacity from any GHG requirements—at facilities that include the coal-fueled ethanol plants. Ironically, ethanol advocates, including the Bush administration, continued to claim GHG reductions of 20 percent or greater from corn ethanol use while promoting their 20-in-10 program.[17]

U.S. Government Findings of GHG Savings Relied on False Assumptions

The claim of 20 percent savings was made throughout the legislative process for both the Energy Policy Act of 2005 and the EISA 2007. The basis for the claim came from statements by the DoE, EPA, and DoA. According to the DoE, the consumption of ethanol from corn would result in about a 20 percent reduction in GHG emissions, compared to gasoline on a life-cycle basis.[18] On the same basis, the EPA claimed that E85 (ethanol blended with 85 percent gasoline) would reduce life-cycle GHG emissions by 15 to 20 percent.[19] Both of those agencies based their claims on estimates from a study the DoA published in 1999, using the

GREET model of the Argonne National Laboratory.[20] A more recent version of the GHG-savings analysis, published in 2007, continued to assume the 20 percent savings.[21]

The government findings of major GHG savings for corn ethanol use under the 2007 legislation depend on four broad assumptions, all of which are flawed:

- An evaluation of the savings based on a relatively modest renewable-fuels standard for corn ethanol—only 4 billion gallons annually.

- An assumption that very little new land would need to be brought under cultivation to supply the additional corn, based on the underlying assumption of a large increase in corn production yields—which did not account for lost corn exports from the higher corn yields that would have decreased foreign CO_2 emissions associated with reduced land-use changes outside the U.S. market.

- An assumption that denitrification—the release of the greenhouse gas nitrous oxide from corn fertilizing activity—was a low 2 percent of fertilizer applied.

- A calculation of savings relative to gasoline that did not adequately address the fossil-fuel requirements of corn transport and ethanol distillation.

Setting the Wrong Baseline for GHG Savings. For its analysis, the DoA assumed an RFS for ethanol of only 4 billion gallons a year by 2010. That number is a modest fraction of the mandated 7.5 billion gallons enacted in 2005 and the 15 billion enacted in 2007. The difference is important because corn yields do not hold constant as increasingly poorer quality and more distant lands are brought into cultivation—or they cannot remain constant without increasing agricultural investment and/or suffering incidental environmental degradation.

The significance of that difference in RFS assumptions is underscored by a simple illustration. Assuming an average corn yield per acre of 160 bushels and about 2.8 gallons of ethanol per bushel, production of 15 billion gallons of ethanol in 2015 would require cultivation of about 34 million acres for corn. That compares with only about 9.4 million acres that was assumed for the 4 billion-gallon ethanol mandate—an increase in land use of over 350 percent in the next seven years. In 2007, nearly 94 million acres were cultivated in the United States for grain corn, the second-highest level on record.

That fact alone offers a compelling reason to revisit and revise the earlier GHG savings estimate. As required by the EISA, the EPA has completed an update in its effort to finalize a regulation to implement the revised RFS provisions of the 2007 legislation. The proposed regulation and supporting analyses were released for public comment in May 2009, and the revised GHG estimates receive a preliminary assessment later in this chapter.

Indirect Increases in Land-Use Release of GHG. The DoA study of GHG savings included only a very small estimate—1 percent of the total ethanol related emissions for the impact of changes in land use attributable to the extra corn production needed to produce 4.0 billion gallons of ethanol. The study assumed an increase of 57 grams per bushel of corn used in ethanol production for indirect land-use changes. That estimate is likely to be low for a number of reasons.[22]

Indirect land-use changes occur when agricultural lands are diverted from producing food and other industrial products to turning out fuel and as fallow lands are brought into service. Somewhere, whether here or abroad, a combination of new land cultivation and/or more intensive cultivation of existing lands is necessary to meet the major increase in demand for corn. The changes are especially important to consider when U.S. corn-ethanol demand is satisfied by a reduction in corn exports, since the yields in other corn-supplying countries are typically 30 to 50 percent lower than here. New corn production in those countries requires much more land.

The now-idle acreage that would be cultivated could include existing forests, ranges, and savannahs, as well as government-owned lands now set aside under the Conservation Reserve Program. Along with the burning of trees, shrubs, and grasses, plus the clearing that is now underway, the new cultivation will immediately release large amounts of carbon dioxide, which the freshly planted corn crops will not totally absorb for many years or decades.

Any prospect for a net reduction in GHG emissions from new corn-ethanol production would then rely on the difference between the immediate GHG increases and the long-term accumulation of net savings from ethanol use relative to gasoline. As a result of the large initial spike in CO_2

emissions that stem from indirect land-use changes owing to the replacement of corn used for ethanol, the new corn-ethanol production will initially increase actual atmospheric CO_2 levels for many years, until small and incremental GHG reductions from future production eventually offset the spike.

Nitrogen Used in Fertilizers Also Creates Greenhouse Gases. A third factor with the potential to significantly raise—perhaps double—the estimates of GHG emissions from corn ethanol production is the process of denitrification. That is the release of nitrous oxide (N_2O) into the atmosphere as fertilizer used for corn production breaks down in the soil. The rate of denitrification measures the percentage change in the degrading of nitrogen into nitrous oxide. Denitrification is important because nitrous oxide has a GHG reactive factor that is 296 times that of carbon dioxide.

From 1975 to 2005, the average use of nitrogen fertilizers on U.S. farms increased by almost one third.[23] Over that same period, corn production yields nearly doubled, but only partly because of increased fertilization. Improved varieties of corn seeds and changes in other farming practices, such as pesticide use and irrigation, are likely to have contributed more to those increased yields. It is unclear how much more new seed research and improved practices can add in the future. Recent investigations by researchers Keeney and Hertel suggest that the national average corn yield could increase by about 30 bushels per acre over a five-year period in response to higher prices resulting from increased demand for biofuel.[24]

This suggests that recent yields in the national average bushels per acre of about 150 would increase to nearly

200 bushels per acre in five or so years. However, the first RFS specified a 2012 level of 7.5 billion gallons. This was increased to 15 billion gallons by 2015. Between 2005 and 2007, the RFS quantity doubled while average corn yields from 2005–08 increased a mere 4 percent, even though corn prices on average also doubled. The theory that much of the increase in ethanol production could be met by increased corn-production yields appears seriously overstated.

Going forward, with continuing depletion of nitrates in currently cultivated lands and increasingly poor soils coming into use, the importance of fertilization is likely to increase. It is uncertain at best that the yield rates suggested by Keeney and Hertel will also increase; scant evidence to date supports the idea that they will.

Documentation for the GREET model indicates a denitrification assumption of 2 percent[25]—the rate assumed by the International Panel on Climate Change (IPCC). However, research by the Nobel Laureate Paul J. Crutzen concludes that the actual rate may be between 3 and 5 percent, twice the level assumed by the IPCC, DoA, and Argonne National Laboratory.[26] On its own, that change in the DoA's denitrification assumption may be enough to turn the overall GHG impacts negative for corn ethanol. In that case, ethanol would increase GHG emissions compared to petroleum gasoline before the increased GHG emissions for indirect land use are taken into account.

Similarly, James N. Galloway, a University of Virginia environmental scientist, concludes that nitrogen is accumulating in the planet's soil, water, and air at an alarming rate that could be detrimental to humans and ecosystems.[27] Galloway's co-author, Alan Townsend of the University of

Colorado, points out that much of the increase is driven by increasing agriculture demands. Other experts disagree with that finding.

Clearly, more research is needed here. But the uncertainty about denitrification is too important to ignore, as it was in the debate over a corn ethanol mandate in 2005 and 2007. In its proposed-regulation materials published in May 2009, the EPA acknowledged that the denitrification issue requires more research, and when it is done, the agency says, assumptions will be adjusted accordingly.

Fossil-Fuel Consumption for Corn and Ethanol Production. The early studies of greenhouse gas emissions related to new ethanol production generally predicted GHG savings, principally because the carbon dioxide released from burning ethanol is largely in balance with the carbon dioxide captured and removed from the atmosphere by growing corn. But specific assumptions about the energy requirements of corn and ethanol production, as well as the choice of fuels, can have a big impact on the associated emissions of GHG—as a full accounting of their effects must acknowledge. Here, too, federal research has overstated the benefits from ethanol use.

All the steps required to produce ethanol consume energy, and for the most part, the energy used has been in the form of fossil fuels. Corn has to be planted, harvested, and transported to ethanol distilleries. After the distillation process, the ethanol has to be taken to a facility that will blend it with gasoline.

Even though producing corn and ethanol and transporting ethanol to blending points would produce significant

GHG emissions, the DoA study concluded that much of ethanol's advantage would be retained. But changes in assumptions about which fossil fuels are consumed in ethanol plants are important; so, too, are assumptions about how far corn and ethanol must be transported. For example, most of the early life-cycle studies found that replacing gasoline with ethanol made from corn would result in some GHG savings, except for instances in which coal was used for process heat—in which case there would be none. As ethanol is more widely blended in gasoline (well beyond its current market in the Midwest), the energy-transportation requirements will exceed the DoA's assumptions.

University Studies and the DoA's Own Work Undermine Federal Claims

The research at Princeton, Minnesota, and elsewhere also challenged the earlier government findings on greenhouse gas savings. It confirmed that GHG emissions from the use of corn ethanol are likely to increase, not decrease, if indirect changes in land use are adequately accounted for.[28] Although that research may not provide the last word on indirect land-use changes, it provides especially important insights into GHG savings estimates by estimating the indirect land-use impacts of higher mandated levels for corn ethanol in 2015:

Princeton University. The first study was prepared by Princeton's Timothy Searchinger (lead author), using a worldwide agricultural model to estimate the indirect land-use effects of the ethanol mandates.[29] His study concluded that "corn based ethanol, instead of producing a 20 percent savings, nearly doubles greenhouse gas emissions over 30 years compared to gasoline and raises emissions of greenhouse gasses for 167 years."

In the study's modeling, the increase is mainly caused by the release of carbon when forests or grasslands worldwide are converted into cropland to produce food to compensate for the diversion of U.S. corn production to fuel ethanol. A second cause of the increase is the loss of carbon sequestration that occurs when the land is converted to crops; at that point, it no longer serves as a carbon repository, which it was in its original state.

The Princeton undertaking employed an updated, worldwide equilibrium model to project changes in cropland acres, and was used to simulate the impacts of an increase in ethanol levels to nearly 30 billion gallons by 2016—a level twice the 2007 RFS mandate. Why the higher level was assumed has not been adequately explained by the researchers, but appears to have been done to better delineate the indirect land-use effects in various parts of the world. Estimated GHG emissions were based on the type of land projected for conversion, including growing or mature forests, grasslands, and savannahs.

Among the key findings:

+ U.S. exports of major crops decline as more corn is diverted to ethanol.

+ As ethanol demand for corn increases, lands now used for soybeans and wheat are switched to corn, and prices increase substantially for all three crops.

+ All but a small percentage of the diverted corn is replaced by increased food production.

+ When other countries replace U.S. exports of corn, farmers abroad must cultivate more acres because their crop yields are lower than ours.

The increase in cultivated acres could occur in a number of countries, including Brazil, China, India, and the United States. The study made adjustments for the GHG releases involving different categories of newly cultivated lands, and sensitivity analyses were completed to gauge higher yields, lower carbon releases for new cropland, and improved technology. Across the board, the results were consistent: negative GHG emissions for at least 30 years.

University of Minnesota. This study was produced by the university in concert with the Nature Conservancy, and was co-authored by Joe Farigone and others.[30] Their findings approximated those of Princeton: ". . . many biofuels—seen by many as potentially low carbon energy sources—actually emit more greenhouse gases than the fossil fuels they aim to replace." Further, "converting rainforests, peat lands, savannas, or grasslands creates a biofuel carbon debt by releasing 17 to 420 times more carbon dioxide than the fossil fuels they replace."

The Minnesota study directly assessed the current U.S. mandate of 15 billion gallons by 2015. Unlike the Princeton research, it did not employ a world equilibrium model, nor were projections of food price or production levels based on the changes caused by the ethanol mandate. However, the study did assess the types of land that would be used to offset corn diversion on a worldwide basis, and it estimated the GHG releases from each type assuming conversion to cropland.

Shortcomings of Initial DoA Work Underscored. The findings highlight the importance of accounting for indirect land-use changes, in conjunction with reasonable assumptions about changes in crop yields, farm uses of fossil fuels and fertilizers, and the fossil-fuel requirements of corn production, transportation, and distillation. Comments on that research indicate that it may prove to be the final word on greenhouse gas emissions, and the weaknesses of the DoA studies that helped promote the new ethanol policy seem clear. Recent comments from the department appear to support that view.

The new studies have drawn some criticism, however. It has been noted that the Princeton findings rely on assumptions for increases in corn yields that may be too low. For example, extending the historical trend points to yields that are 30 percent higher than the baseline yield the Princeton researchers assumed.[31] But a higher yield of that magnitude would necessarily come with large increases in the use of nitrogen fertilizer, and the Princeton paper did not include an assessment of the related GHG impacts of that denitrification.

A letter from the authors of the original DoA study (Michael Wang and Zia Hua) to *Science* magazine, commenting on the Princeton research, acknowledged that their assumption of a renewable fuels standard of only 4 billion gallons by

2010 is outdated. But the authors criticized the study on a number of points:[32]

+ The assumed mandate of 30 billion gallons (which may have overstated land-use changes).

+ The lack of a clear baseline assumption for global food supply (which makes it difficult to assess the extent of crop diversion).

+ The assumptions on crop yields from the newly culti-vated lands (which may be too low).

Those criticisms notwithstanding, the DoA's earlier research is obsolete and inaccurate, and the department has never provided a valid analytic basis for the claims of 20-percent GHG savings for the levels specified by either the 2005 or 2007 acts. Substantially higher future corn yields may re-duce the indirect land-use impacts, but that assumption ap-pears very optimistic. The subject needs further study—ex-tended to cover the separate GHG impacts of the increased nitrogen fertilization necessary to boost yields.

Both the California Air Resources board and the EPA have undertaken what appear to be extensive analyses of the indirect land-use impact of the RFS policy and the related GHG effects. A sound methodology is needed in order to make informed decisions about the policy. However, at this point the question is not whether there are impacts but the magnitude of them. Enough research has been done to confirm that major GHG-related emissions result from indirect land-use changes at an RFS level of 15 billion gallons. The likely end result: GHG emission impacts for corn ethanol-blended gasoline that are negative compared to petroleum gasoline— or at least no better using a reasonable amortized basis.[33]

But perhaps the most telling point from the Wang-Hua letter is the disclosure that the GHG emissions from land use in the current GREET model need to be updated. (Various organizations have recently begun to do so.) That forthright acknowledgement is disconcerting, because it strongly suggests that the U.S. government had no idea whether corn ethanol would actually result in GHG emission savings at the 7.5-billion *or* the 15-billion-gallon annual mandated level.

EPA's 2009 Proposed Rulemaking to Implement Energy Independence and Security Act Changes to the RFS

The 549-page proposed rule and its supporting documents constitute a first step in implementing the GHG savings standards for the various forms of biofuels covered under EISA.[34] For corn ethanol, the act requires that all future plants achieve at least 20-percent GHG savings compared to petroleum gasoline, taking into account both direct and indirect GHG emissions. The minimum savings for the more advanced biofuels, such as cellulose ethanol, is far greater than for corn ethanol.

Because the proposed rule and its related documentation appeared when this book was in final manuscript form, there was insufficient time for a thorough and detailed assessment. But a preliminary review indicated that the EPA analysis in the proposed rule generally confirms the findings of the Princeton and Minnesota studies. When the indirect effects are taken into account, corn ethanol made from using natural gas as the plant fuel does not result in significant GHG savings and does not meet the 20-percent saving standard specified in the act. Further, ethanol plants using coal for plant fuel actually increase GHG emissions compared to petroleum gasoline by as much as 34 percent.

The good news is that nearly four years after the first RFS was enacted, the government has finally completed a reasonably comprehensive assessment of the GHG impacts of the various types of plant technologies in current use to make corn ethanol. Ironically, nearly 15.4 billion gallons of plant capacity have been built (13.4 billion gallons) or are under construction (2 billion gallons), so the EPA analysis comes largely after the fact.[35] U.S. consumers and taxpayers have been misled by earlier claims that corn ethanol achieves a 20-percent GHG savings compared to petroleum gasoline. It does not.

But the EPA, whose mission is to protect the environment, is hedging on its GHG-impacts analysis for corn ethanol. The agency has put forth two methods of estimating the indirect effects. The first uses a thirty-year period to amortize the indirect GHG release when other countries' non-agricultural land is cultivated to make up for the loss in corn for feed that is diverted to making corn ethanol. When this new land is cultivated, a major release of GHG becomes associated with the initial year of the biofuel production. The second option uses a one hundred-year amortization period with a minor (2 percent) discount for future GHG changes.

The supporting rationale put forth in the EPA proposed regulation amounts to analytic drivel, not substantive justification, and should be dropped from the final rule. The methodology of amortizing the biofuel emission over a long future period of time is essentially an accounting trick to mask the large increase in GHG emissions during the early years of corn ethanol expansion. The actual increase in GHG associated with the substance is illustrated in Figure 4.1, which is the EPA's own chart for the corn ethanol life cycle of GHG emissions over time.[36]

The EPA's analysis for corn ethanol shows that a real net reduction of cumulative GHGs in the atmosphere does not begin to occur until thirty-three years after the program is

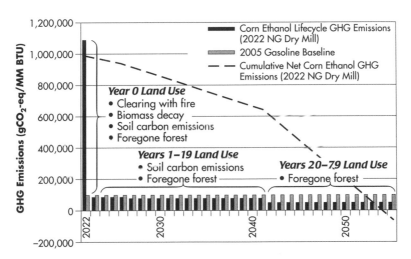

FIGURE 4.1 Corn Ethanol Lifecycle GHG Emissions over Time and Payback Period

Sources: "Regulation of Fuels and Fuel Additives: Changes to Renewable Fuels Standard Program," EPA, HQ-OAR-2005-0161; RIN 2060-A081, EPA, NOPR, May 5, 2009.

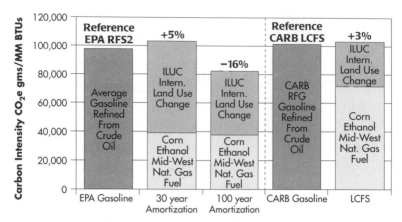

FIGURE 4.2 Fuel GHG Emissions: Gasoline vs. Corn Ethanol

Sources: "Regulation of Fuels and Fuel Additives: Changes to Renewable Fuels Standard Program," EPA-HQ-OAR-2005-0161; RIN 2060-A081, Environmental Protection Agency, "Notice of Proposed Rulemaking," May 5, 2009, p. 315; California Environmental Protection Agency/Air Resources Board, "Proposed Regulation to Implement the Low Carbon Fuel Standard," Volume I, Staff Report: Initial Statement of Reasons, Release Date: March 5, 2009.

fully implemented (in 2055). Even though the analysis shows that the expansion of corn ethanol creates large increases in GHG emissions, the agency's proposed accounting methodologies mask those initial increases—as illustrated by the "normalized" carbon intensities of the fuels shown in Figure 4.2. (They are based on information developed by the EPA.[37])

For comparison, Figure 4.2 also includes the carbon intensities for the same fuels as adopted by the California Air Resource Board for its low-carbon fuel-standard program. That program employed a similar amortization method to mask or dilute the initial spike in GHG emissions for corn ethanol. Even so, the analysis using the shorter amortizations for both the EPA and the California board show that corn ethanol produces more GHG emissions than the fossil gasoline energy it will be replacing. The comparison in Figure 4.2 also raises a separate analytical issue, since EPA's GHG intensity for the corn ethanol process excluding the indirect land-use change emissions is much lower than estimated by CARB. Both use the same process and source in their analyses. The analyses were done separately.

A more environmentally sound approach would use an even-shorter amortization period than the thirty years the EPA is proposing in the final rule. The reason is that the House Energy and Commerce Committee approved, in May 2009, a GHG cap-and-trade bill that mandates a 17 percent reduction of total GHG emissions below 2005 levels by 2020 and an 83 percent reduction by 2050. As the EPA analysis in Figure 4.1 shows, any new corn-ethanol production in the near future will not begin providing GHG reductions until after 2055. The EPA's proposed one hundred-year amortization method would use estimated GHG reductions from today's new corn-ethanol plants as far as 2122 in the future to make the new corn ethanol appear to be reducing GHGs today. It is no wonder why the House Agriculture Committee leadership fought and got a provision in this bill that would prohibit EPA from taking into account indirect land use effects in estimating GHG emissions for corn ethanol.

The EPA makes the absurd implied assumption that vehicles a century from now will still be fueled with ethanol-blended gasoline. Peak crude-oil production is likely to occur many decades before 2122; and vehicles are very likely to be electrified in the next 50 years, based on the highly aggressive CAFE standards—an average of 39 miles per gallon by 2016—that were strongly supported by EPA.

Since corn ethanol is mandated, deeply subsidized, and trade protected by the U.S. government, shouldn't it be required to produce substantial GHG savings that contribute to meeting the mandated GHG reduction requirements of 17 percent by 2020 and 83 percent by 2050? Why would it make sense to build more corn ethanol plants when the evidence shows a surge in GHG emissions the day such a plant begins production?

Advocates might argue that the indirect GHG emissions from a new ethanol plant would occur in other countries (indirect land-use effects) and that, on a strictly U.S. accounting basis, emissions for a new state-of-the-art, natural gas-fired ethanol plant may meet a 10-percent savings standard if the EPA established it. Such an argument ignores the fact that the United States will play a lead role internationally in convincing and cajoling other major GHG-emitting nations to adopt a policy like the bill approved by the House committee. How can our country be successful if those nations know that U.S. corn-ethanol policy is sharply increasing their GHG emissions because of their indirect effects?

In sum, what is now known about GHG emissions from corn ethanol shows conclusively that, compared to petroleum gasoline, corn ethanol does not reduce emissions. As an alternative to corn ethanol, the EPA's analysis suggests that advanced biofuels from cellulose biomass (such as switchgrass) may provide large reductions in GHG emissions from transportation fuels—if the technology hurdles of the cellulose process are overcome. However, growing the biomass for biofuels, like growing corn itself, will consume similarly large amounts of agricultural resources—e.g., arable land and water supplies—that we use for food.

Building an Infrastructure for Real BioFuel

Investments to Produce Corn and Distill Corn Ethanol Will Not Help Jump Start a Cellulose Ethanol Industry. As environmentalists and policymakers learn more about corn ethanol's environmental shortfalls, the justifying argument has been revised. It now suggests that the use of corn-based ethanol represents a necessary intermediate bridging strategy to achieve the next generation of biofuels that will provide "real" greenhouse gas reductions.

The bridging argument is built into the ethanol-mandate schedule of EISA 2007. The first wave of required renewable fuel use will be mostly corn-based ethanol (a conventional renewable fuel), which is then effectively capped at 15 billion gallons per year by 2015. The remaining 21 billion gallons per year of renewable fuels by 2022 is supposed to be satisfied with yet-to-be-commercialized advanced biofuels (such as cellulose ethanol) that should provide actual greenhouse-gas reductions. The EIA concludes that the cellulose RFS-mandated quantities will not be met by 2022 but probably by 2030.[38]

A further important reason why the claim is not valid is the "blend wall," the current 10 percent limit on the ethanol content of gasoline. This limit will be reached in the 2009–10 timeframe when corn ethanol reaches 11–12 billion gallons annually. This means that as cellulose ethanol production increases, there will not be room to blend it with gasoline unless the E10 (10 percent ethanol-blended gasoline) limit is increased. EPA has under review a waiver to the limit that would allow E15 blending or 15 percent ethanol. The auto manufacturers and many others have mounted formidable opposition to any increase to the E10 level.

Corn ethanol poses a serious competitive threat to cellulose ethanol and should be viewed as such. It is not, as some claim, building the infrastructure for a 36 billion gallon–per-year ethanol industry. Even if the 10 percent is increased to 15 percent, the result would amount to less than 20 billion gallons per year of ethanol blending.

Does Ethanol-Blended Gasoline Improve Local Air Quality?

Ethanol Contributes to Smog and the Release of Known Carcinogens. Ethanol advocates claim that ethanol-blended gasoline reduces vehicle emissions and therefore benefits the environment. The primary focus of those claims is on carbon monoxide emissions, which can be lower with oxygenate fuels. However, other emissions can increase. In particular, light-duty vehicles fueled with an ethanol blend emit significantly higher levels of acetaldehyde and probably formaldehyde, both known carcinogens. Because of the lighter vapor pressure of ethanol blends, evaporative emissions of other dangerous compounds during refueling are also higher. Those additional emissions can increase smog formation and cause numerous health concerns. None of those potentially adverse impacts were addressed in determining ethanol-mandate quantities for the Energy Independence and Security Act of 2007.

A major goal of the Clean Air Act is to reduce all vehicle emissions that contribute to the formation of ozone, a lung-irritating air pollutant, during hot summer days. The emission precursors of ozone are VOCs (volatile organic compounds), NO_x (nitrogen oxides) and CO (carbon monoxide). Vehicle VOCs are emitted by two sources: tailpipe exhaust and gasoline vapors that leak from the vehicle's fuel system. In general, evaporative emissions will represent one-quarter to one-third of total vehicle VOCs.

Adding oxygenates (such as MTBE and ethanol) to gasoline is known to reduce exhaust emissions of CO and VOCs in older vehicles with less-efficient fuel systems, by adding more oxygen during combustion. This reduction in older vehicles is the main reason why the fuel-oxygen standard became part of the RFG (reformulated gasoline) requirement in the 1990 Clean Air Act Amendments. (Ethanol mandates rendered the oxygenate requirement redundant, and it was eliminated in 2006.) However, that same increase in gasoline oxygen content contributes to increases in NO_x emissions from combustion. When more ethanol is blended into gasoline, therefore, the result is an environmental tradeoff: NO_x increases, and exhaust VOC decreases.

In addition to increasing exhaust emissions of NO_x, adding ethanol to gasoline raises its vapor pressure and contributes to about 25 percent more evaporative VOC emissions (based on the EPA's RFG Complex Model, which is used to predict vehicle emissions). Refiners can adjust the other components of their gasoline to help offset that increase. Unfortunately, the adjustment to the gasoline formula involves displacing low-cost butane, which incrementally comes from lower cost natural gas supplies. That is, managing the impact of ethanol's high vapor pressure again requires a tradeoff, this time between (1) increased evaporative VOC emissions and higher air pollution and (2) increased crude-oil consumption for gasoline production because of the removal of some of the low-cost, butane-blended into gasoline to meet the requirement.

Although adding ethanol reduces exhaust CO and VOCs in vehicles built in the 1980s and '90s, a recent study conducted for California by the Coordinating Research Council (CRC) found that adding ethanol provides no benefit in reducing exhaust VOCs in newer vehicles, but does contribute to increased NO_x emissions and air toxic emissions.[39] The study conducted exhaust-emission tests on twelve 2001-to-2003 low-emission vehicles with fuels containing zero, 5.7, and 10.0 percent ethanol for different gasoline distillation-volatility properties. Those fuels reflected the range of choices in the California RFG program. The emission results shown in Figure 4.3, taken from the report,

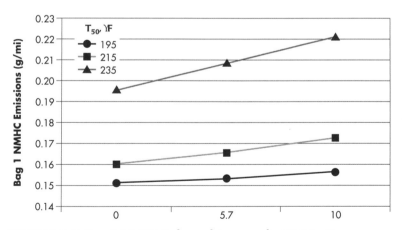

FIGURE 4.3 Bag 1 NMHC Balanced Average by RtOH x T_{50}

Source: Coordinating Research Council (CRC), "Effects of Ethanol and Volatility Parameters on Exhaust Emissions," Project Report No.E-67.

demonstrate that adding ethanol to gasoline increases exhaust NMHC emissions (non-methane hydrocarbons) for all distillation volatilities. The statistics from the study show an average 6-percent increase in exhaust NMHC for 10-percent ethanol blends with newer vehicles. (However, the statistical strength for this estimate is slightly less than statistically significant.)

As observed with older vehicles, Figure 4.4, from the CRC study, shows that adding 10 percent ethanol to gasoline also increases NO_x emissions. The study shows an average 5-percent increase in NO_x when 10 percent ethanol was added to the gasoline.

The same study, measuring four airborne toxics in the exhaust emissions of a subset of vehicles, found that adding

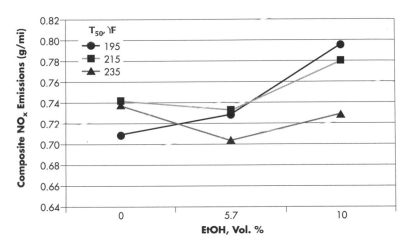

FIGURE 4.4 Composite NO_x Balanced Average EtOH x T_{50} Fleet Average

Source: CRC, "Effects of Ethanol and Volatility Parameters on Exhaust Emissions," Project Report No. E-67.

ethanol significantly increased emissions of all four (benzene, butadiene, formaldehyde, and acetaldehyde).

Therefore, unlike many prior fuel-emission studies conducted with pre-2000 vehicles, this more recent CRC study suggests that newer model vehicles (2001–03) may not realize a reduction in exhaust VOCs with ethanol blends, and may even contribute to an increase in exhaust VOC emissions and possibly air-toxics emissions as well. However, like the prior studies, this one by the CRC reconfirms that adding 10 percent ethanol to the fuel will increase NO_x emissions by about 5 percent. While the CRC study focused on the impact of ethanol-blend pollutants in the exhaust emissions, another CRC study, conducted for California, focused on the impact of blends on the evaporative emissions.[40]

Until recently, the EPA and the CARB both assumed that ethanol blends perform like all other types of gasoline (both hydrocarbon and MTBE blends) when it came to vehicle-evaporative emissions. That is, they assumed that such emissions from vehicles are only a function of the gasoline's volatility (mostly RVP) and are not related to the fuel used in the gasoline. However, evaporative emission studies in the early 2000s proved that assumption false for ethanol blends, which turned out to contribute to increased evaporative emissions via increased VOC permeation through the rubber and elastomer parts used in vehicle fuel systems.

Drawing on the CRC's results, the CARB estimated that using ethanol blends at all commercial concentrations (5 to 10 percent) has been significantly increasing their VOC inventory via increased VOC permeation from the vehicle fuel systems: "This represents a seven percent increase in

evaporative emissions and a four percent increase in overall hydrocarbon (HC) emissions."[41] To compensate for this
previously unknown amount of additional permeation, the
CARB developed and issued a new reformulated gasoline
regulation, which required that refiners make additional
costly fuel changes to compensate for the increased emissions associated with ethanol blends.[42]

An alternative being promoted to displace gasoline re-
fined from crude oil is the E85 fuel mixture. That blend can
only be used in flexible-fuel vehicles, with systems specifically
designed to run on either the mixture or gasoline. There are
only about six million such vehicles on the road of more than
230 million in all. In addition to requiring enhanced fuel
systems, E85 distribution requires the installation of separate dispenser pumps that are compatible with high ethanol-
content fuel. Although E85 is also promoted by ethanol
advocates, a 2006 health risk study conducted at Stanford found
that the widespread use of E85 to replace gasoline will contribute to an increase in ozone and ozone-related deaths.[43]

Water Scarcity and Water Quality: Unintended Consequences

Growing more corn for ethanol is having unfavorable impacts on the nation's fresh water supplies and water quality.
Fresh water is a growing national problem, straining compet-
ing agricultural interests and pitting farms against industries
and cities. The problem is especially acute in Midwestern
corn-growing areas that rely on aquifers. Corn uses more

water than most crops, and ethanol operations add to the demand. In addition to water-supply issues, the fertilizer requirements of corn production are leading to contamination of local groundwater and streams, and also contributing to oxygen depletion and formation of dead zones in the Gulf of Mexico, near the mouth of the Mississippi River.

Water Scarcity is a Growing U.S. Problem. Because growing food and livestock is so water intensive, the scarcity of fresh water looms as a major issue around the globe. Crop irrigation and livestock use are estimated to account for 84 percent of U.S. water consumption. But the measurement for agriculture does not include the large amount of rainwater—used for growing corn—that would otherwise flow directly into aquifers or dams, lakes, and rivers. The U.S. Government Accountability Office reported, in a 2003 survey of states, that under normal weather conditions over the next ten years, officials in thirty-six states expect to see water shortages. (See Figure 4.5 below)

A DoE report to Congress stresses that "available surface water supplies have not increased in 20 years, and groundwater tables and supplies are dropping at an alarming rate."[44] Because of growing water consumption, many large rivers flowing to the coastal water bodies in the western U.S. have flows that are barely sufficient during summer to reach the ocean.

The large "eight state" (Ogallala) aquifer, which provides much of the Midwest with water, continues its unsustainable decline in water levels. Battles over water rights, which are common in the western half of the country, are now spreading to areas around the Great Lakes and in the Southeast.

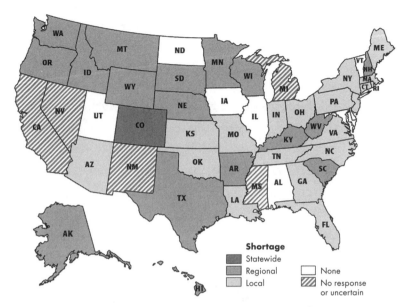

FIGURE 4.5 Survey of Likely Water Shortages over the Next Decade under Average Conditions

Source: DoE, "Energy Demands on Water Resources, Report to Congress on the Interdependency of Energy and Water," December 2006.

Because of the growing uncertainty over fresh-water sup-plies flowing from the inland regions of the country, many large population areas on the coasts are building or consider-ing costly saltwater-desalination plants, which are also very energy intensive.

Water Consumption for Growing Corn to Produce Eth-anol. As the largest U.S. crop, corn plays a significant role in the availability of fresh-water supplies, and uses the most land use of all the nation's agricultural products. About 20

percent of all corn planted is irrigated. Since it is also the most fertilizer-intensive crop, its expanded production for biofuel has raised concerns regarding water supplies and water quality. Like other food crops and biomass, growing corn consumes large amounts of fresh-water, via evaporation and transpiration, during its growing season. The Food and Agriculture Organization estimates that corn consumes about 75 gallons of water per pound of corn (1.6 kg of corn per cubic meter of water) during the season.[45] Others have estimated that growing more corn for ethanol will significantly drain inland fresh-water supplies.

On an ethanol basis, the total amount of rain and irrigation water consumed for growing corn crops ranges from 1,100 gallon of water per one gallon of ethanol for Iowa to as high as 1,500 gallons of water in Nebraska.[46] Using the lower estimate, producing 15 billion gallons per year of ethanol from domestic corn will use up 16.5 trillion gallons of water per year. That hidden water consumption for ethanol fuel is equal to about 150 gallons of water per day per person in the nation—an amount half again as large as the 100 gallons of daily household water a person typically uses.

Such a large increase in water consumption to meet the corn ethanol mandate will reduce the normal amount of inland flow to the coasts via underground aquifers and surface waters. Of course, some of that increased agricultural-water demand for domestic biofuels can be indirectly "exported" to other countries by diverting a portion of the nation's exports of food crops (or meats grown on corn) to domestic biofuel production. That would pressure other countries to use their fresh-water supplies to grow more crops. Because of the growing global scarcity of those supplies, the global trade in food crops to some extent rebalances fresh-water supplies because countries with available supplies can increase their production and exports to countries with less water availability. This has become known as "virtual water."[47]

Water Consumption for Operating Ethanol Plants

As with most energy-processing facilities, ethanol plants consume a significant amount of water—generally between 3 to 5 gallons for every gallon of ethanol produced. Although that is not nearly the amount needed to grow the corn for the ethanol plant, the annual water demands of a new plant that produces 100 million gallons of corn ethanol per year would be as much as 500 million gallons. Such a plant drawing from public water systems in rural areas could easily overwhelm supplies available to nearby communities. For example, one new ethanol plant can consume as much water as a town of 5,000 people. For that reason, from Minnesota to Florida to California, local communities have rejected a number of proposed ethanol plants in the past few years.[48]

No other form of energy is nearly so intensive in water consumption as growing biocrops and processing ethanol from corn. That result was documented in a DoE report, delivered to the Congress in late 2006.[49] Because of the growing national concern that energy processing and expanding production might be straining the nation's fresh-water resources, Congress had instructed the department to review the connection between energy demands and water demands.

Although much of the report focuses on electric power generation, it also addresses transportation fuels, including biofuels and the crops that provide the raw material for them. Figure 4.6, from the report, compares the water-consumption requirements with the product's energy content (measured in gallons of water per million BTUs) for various crops and energy sources. (To cover the wide range of water usages, consumption is shown on a log scale with orders of magnitude.)

For reasons discussed earlier, the irrigation water for growing biocrops such as soybeans and corn consumes more

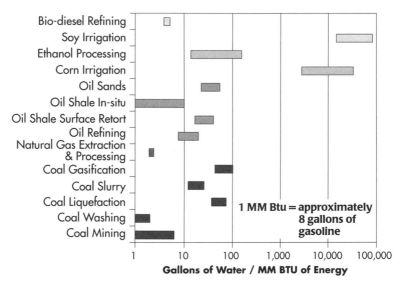

FIGURE 4.6 Water Consumption per MM BTUs of Energy by Technology Type

Source: DoE, "Energy Demands on Water Resources," "Report to Congress on the Interdependency of Energy and Water," December 2006.

water (about 10,000 gallons per million BTUs for corn ethanol) than any of the other processes for producing transportation energy. Even the measurements of large water usage
for irrigation understates the total amount of water consumed when growing those crops, since much of the rain is
also captured by the corn plants instead of flowing into underground aquifers or surface waters, where it is available for
other uses. But the corn-to-ethanol conversion process also
consumes a great deal of water (about 50 gallons per million
BTUs—roughly five times as much as refining crude oil into
gasoline or diesel).

Water-Quality Risks from Corn Production

Of all the major food and industrial crops, corn is probably
the most nutrient intensive, depleting the earth of nitrogen and therefore requiring heavy applications of nitrogen
fertilizers. Nitrogen for growing corn in the United States
commonly calls for 150 pounds per acre. Of that amount, perhaps only 50 to 60 percent is consumed by the corn plant
and hauled off the farm, with the remainder lost to the surrounding environment.

In addition to the portion that is oxidized as nitrous
oxide gas (a potent GHG), a significant portion of the lost
nitrogen works its way into nearby waterways via rain runoff or migration via the aquifers. Once in the waterways
and exposed to sunlight, it can fertilize large algae blooms.
When the blooms die, the algae fall to the lake, river bottom,

or seabed, where, in their decomposed state, they consume nearly all the oxygen in the surrounding water. The consequences of that oxygen depletion can be quite devastating, depending on the amount of nitrogen being supplied. Oxygen-starved waters become "dead zones" for most forms of water life—a condition known as hypoxia.

Nitrogen runoff into the Mississippi River system is known to be the major cause of a dead zone in the Gulf of Mexico, as illustrated in Figure 4.7.[50] In 2007, the hypoxia area along the Gulf Coast reached a near-record 7,700 square miles, larger than the state of New Jersey. With nutrients from the entire U.S. corn belt running into the Mississippi watershed, increasing corn acreage and yields will mean even more nitrogen draining into the gulf.[51]

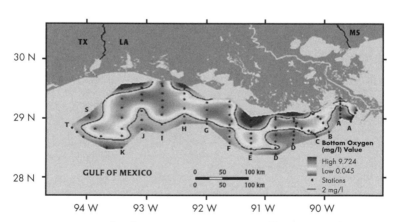

FIGURE 4.7 Dissolved Oxygen Contours (in milligrams per liter) in the Gulf of Mexico, July 21–28, 2007

Source: National Research Council of the National Academies, Committee on Water Implications of Biofuels Production in the United States, "Water Implications of Biofuels Production in the United States," 2007.

Other bodies of water that lie downriver from agriculture regions are experiencing similar problems. Many bodies, like the Chesapeake Bay, also suffer from hypoxia caused by nutrient pollution from fertilizer runoff. Over the past forty years, the volume of the Chesapeake's hypoxic zone has more than tripled, and it may start to cover much of the bay during the summer months. Also, many inland lakes are oxygen starved, generally due to excess levels of phosphorous. As biofuel production increases, overall agricultural production (especially on marginal lands more prone to soil erosion and located near waterways) and fertilizer use will also increase, as will runoff, and all will contribute to the growing deadzone problem.

5

Other Claims: Are Budget Costs Reduced? Is the Trade Balance Improved? Is Rural Employment Increased?

The three major remaining claims by corn ethanol advocates:

+ Federal budget costs will be lower because higher demand for corn will raise corn prices and lower DoA subsidies.

+ The U.S. balance of payment deficit will decline because less petroleum will be imported.

+ Rural employment will increase.

Reduced Federal Budgets?

Summarized in Figure 5.1 are the major federal budget costs for corn, soybean-producer subsidies, and tax subsidies related to ethanol production and use. Because the government has not made a comprehensive estimate of federal budget costs for corn ethanol, Figure 5.1 understates total costs.

	1995–2006	2008–2017	Total/billions
Department of Agriculture and Energy, and the Environmental Protection Agency			
—Various production-related subsidies paid to corn and soybean producers	$70.4[1]	$36.4[2]	$106.8
—Subsidized crop insurance	[3]	30.6[2]	30.6
—Disaster payments to corn and soybean producers[4]	7.6	7.2	14.8
—Estimated cost of to strategic ethanol reserve of 3 billion gallons to mitigate massive corn-price increases due to floods and droughts		10[5]	10
—Other federal ethanol-related programs[6]	Not Avail	Not Avail	Not Avail
Department of Agriculture and Department of Treasury			
—Tax revenues forgone because of the tax credit for ethanol blending in gasoline	17.8	58.8	76.6
—Tax revenues forgone for other ethanol tax subsidies[7]	Not Avail	Not Avail	Not Avail
Total estimated federal taxpayer costs ($ billions):	$95.8	$143	$238.8

Figure 5.1 Estimated U.S. Federal Taxpayer Cost Under the Federal Corn-Ethanol Policy

(*continued*)

Figure 5.1 *(continued)*

Sources/Explanation: [1]Environmental Working Group (EWG) website, www.EWG.org, "Corn, Soybean Commodities Subsidies and Disaster Assistance Payments in the United States," 1995–2006.
[2]Congressional Budget Office (CBO), 2008 Summer Baseline budget estimates.
[3]Included in various production-related subsidies line for 1995–2006.
[4]EWG Website, "Farm Subsidy Database, Commodities Subsidies in the United States," 1995–2006.
[5]Based on DoA, DoE, "Report to Congress on the Feasibility of Including Biomass Fuels as Part of the Strategic Petroleum Reserve," April 2002. For the steel tank storage and maintenance costs: EIA, Annual Energy Outlook 2007. Reference Case was used for ethanol prices that were adjusted for inflation at 2 percent annually.
[6]Other budget costs include: Food and nutrition program increases caused by higher corn prices; Renewable Fuels Standard (RFS) administrative costs; E85 fuel purchases; FFV (flex-fuel vehicles) purchases; grants and loans for various ethanol related purposes; subsidized Rural Utility Service loans for rural power plant and transmission lines, E10 and higher blends research, emissions testing, etc.
[7]Other ethanol tax subsidies, including the E85 retail-distribution pump tax credit and small ethanol-producer tax credit.

As can be seen, the estimated budget costs for the post-RFS period of 2008–2017 (ten years) are about 50 percent higher than for pre-RFS 1995–2006 (eleven years). There are several reasons for this. The first is that the DoA crop subsidy-payments savings claimed by the ethanol advocates are not expected to occur because the corn/soybean growers demanded and got continued payments in the 2007 farm bill. Further, the growers continue to be eligible for heavily subsidized federal-crop insurance, and the budget costs, as estimated by the CBO, are substantial for this subsidy. Second, although Congress reduced the tax subsidy from 51 to 45 cents per gallon in 2007, it remains in effect. The much larger volumes of ethanol required for blending under the RFS drive the budget cost (forgone tax revenues for 2008–2017) up 330 percent over 1995–2006.

Third, the author believes that the government will authorize and build a strategic ethanol reserve when the first major drought occurs under the RFS policy. The 2008–2017 cumulative budgets include the expense of a 3-billion-gallon reserve–at an estimated cost of $10 billion for the period.[52] But even if this cost is omitted, estimated federal budget costs increase nearly 39 percent for 2008–2017 over 1995–2006.

Further, the federal budget costs left out of this comparison—because they are not available for 2008–2017—are significant.[53] The CBO estimated that increased ethanol use accounted for 10–15 percent of the rise in food prices between April 2007 and April 2008. In turn, this caused an estimated increase in federal spending for food and nutrition programs of some $600 to $900 million in fiscal year 2009 alone.

In sum, the major federal budget costs from 1995 to 2006 (2007 was not available) were $95.8 billion, compared to an estimated $143 billion from 2008–2017. Overall, the claim of reduced budget costs is not correct. Under a competitive market policy, those costs would be substantially lower.

Reduce the U.S. Balance-of-Payments Deficit?

In Chapter 3, on petroleum imports, the ethanol policy yielded a net increase in domestically produced ethanol in 2015 of 5.2 billion gallons of domestically produced ethanol. Adjusting for ethanol's lower BTU content, the net petroleum equivalent is 3.5 billion gallons of gasoline equivalent, which equals about $7 billion per year of import expenditures for gasoline at $2 per gallon. Based on EIA figures for 2008, U.S. net petroleum imports in 2015 will be about 192 billion gallons. In comparison, the additional 3.5 billion gallons of ethanol amounts to 1.8 percent of projected 2015 petroleum imports. This is before adjusting for lower U.S. corn and soybean exports and higher U.S. imports of petroleum that is consumed to make and distribute the ethanol. Although a more comprehensive assessment is needed, it is very doubtful that domestic corn ethanol has any positive effect on the U.S. balance of payments.

Increase Rural Employment?

The federal ethanol policy will increase rural employment in the ten Midwestern top corn-and-soybean-producing states. If an average of 200 people are employed at a 100 million gallon per-year corn ethanol plant, 24,000 jobs will be created. In addition, employment will increase in corn production and in the many service-sector jobs related to both it and ethanol production in those rural areas. From that basic perspective, the claim is justified.

But at what price to workers in the many other industries that have to pay all the costs (as shown in Part II, Chapter 6)? These large additional costs imposed on taxpayers and consumers result in fewer jobs elsewhere in the U.S. economy—that could exceed the jobs created in corn-producing states. Even within the farm sector, ethanol policy may lead to job reductions. For example, livestock producers, and presumably the jobs they offered, were adversely impacted by the sharply higher corn prices.

If the U.S. economy were entirely built around federal policies based on quantity mandates, deep production subsidies, and import-protection, the economy would soon become totally uncompetitive in world markets. The highly productive and cost-competitive parts of the economy must generate the wealth necessary to pay for the ethanol policy; otherwise we could not afford it.

6

Who Pays for the Policy, and Who Benefits from It?

Introduction

Federal ethanol policies and programs are diverse, numerous, and costly. They include tax and regulatory subsidies, spending-program subsidies, and import protection. Massive federal intervention in the marketplace is the cornerstone. The end result will be an estimated cost to taxpayers and consumers of about $500 billion from 2008–2017. (See Figure 6.7)

Just who pays for and who benefits from current ethanol policy? The primary payers and beneficiaries are summarized below.

Who Pays?	Who Benefits?
Federal taxpayers	Corn and soybean producers
Gasoline purchasers	Owners of corn and soybean farmland
Food purchasers	Ethanol plant owners and workers
	Petroleum refiners and importers

Estimates of the numbers of payers and beneficiaries and the amounts paid and benefited follow.

Between Two Hundred Million and Three Hundred Million People Pay. In 2008, there were 138 million federal tax returns filed[54] and over 230 million light-duty vehicles on the road, the vast majority of them burning ethanol-blended gasoline.[55] In mid 2008, American food consumers numbered 304 million.[56] Thus, those who pay the ethanol policy-related subsidies number two to three hundred million.

The subsidy costs paid per transaction are small and not traceable to the beneficiaries. There is nothing on retail gasoline pumps, for example, indicating that every gallon of ethanol blended in gasoline receives a 45-cent federal tax subsidy. Further, those who pay often receive erroneous information from the federal government and other involved or interested parties. For example, during the summer of 2008, when gasoline prices rose above $4 per gallon, the DoE published on its website a claim that federal ethanol policies drove retail gasoline prices down between 20 and 35 cents per gallon.[57]

Fortunately, a group within DoE, the Energy Information Administration, is charged by statute with providing the public with factual, objective analyses. And in September 2007, the EIA published a report disclosing that a competitive, market-reliance policy for ethanol (no tax subsidy, no RFS mandate, no import fee) would result in an amount of ethanol being blended into gasoline nearly identical to that generated by the then-current ethanol policy.[58] The DoE claim of a 20–35 cent per-gallon reduction in gasoline prices simply was not true. The ethanol policies could not have resulted in lower gasoline prices, because the RFS-mandated ethanol-blend level for 2008 was the same as the EIA-estimated level that would result under a competitive market policy.[59]

Federal ethanol policies are stealthy. It is impossible for the uninitiated to know how much is being paid, who benefits, and by how much. That information cannot be found in the federal budget or in the hundreds of reports on energy published each year. Even though huge amounts of wealth are being transferred, there is no accountability at the federal level.

In this section, therefore, the author attempts to provide that accountability and to give at least some transparency to federal ethanol policy.

Several Hundred Thousand Corn and Soybean Farms (Operators and Owners), Concentrated in Ten Midwestern States, Are the Prime Beneficiaries

As the highlighting in Figure 6.1 indicates, ten Midwestern states contain the most productive corn and soybean farmland *and* the largest number of harvested acres in the United States. Figure 6.2, a county-level map, shows where the harvested acres are located. Figure 6.3 is an identical map except for showing soybeans, a sister crop to corn; there, too, the ten states have the greatest number of harvested acres.

FIGURE 6.1 Top Ten Corn-, Soybean-, and Ethanol-Producing States

Source: DoA/NASS, "Quick Stats," December 2008.

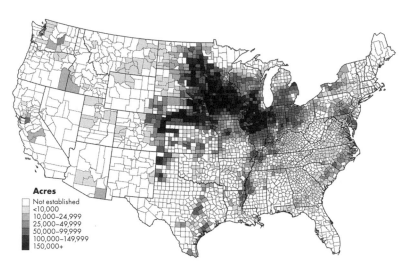

FIGURE 6.2 Harvested Acres of Corn for Grain, by County, 2007

Source: DoA/NASS, "Quick Stats," December 2008.

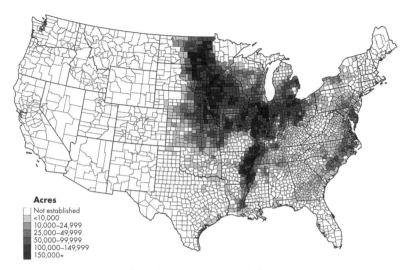

Acres

☐ Not established
< 10,000
10,000–24,999
25,000–49,999
50,000–99,999
100,000–149,999
150,000+

FIGURE 6.3 Acres of Soybeans Harvested, by County, 2007

Source: DoA/NASS, "Quick Stats," December 2008.

How Corn Soybean Farms (Operators and Owners) Reap Substantial Benefits

Background on farm statistics shows the number of farms that benefit the most, and by how much, from federal ethanol policy. In 2002, the latest year available, there were 2,128,982 farms in the United States. According to the DoA's Agriculture Census. (Of these, 348,590, or 16.4, percent, grew corn and 317,611 soybeans. (Since most Midwest corn farms also produce soybeans, the figures include a good deal of double counting.)

To get state-by-state detail, one must use the 2002 Census data for "Number of grains [includes field corn], oil seeds [includes soybeans], dry beans, dry peas," broken down by

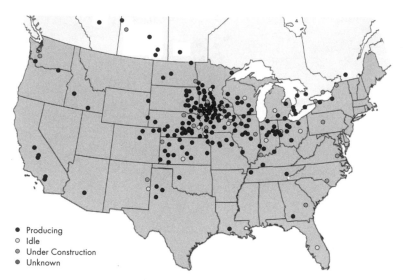

- ● Producing
- ○ Idle
- ◉ Under Construction
- ● Unknown

FIGURE 6.4 Locations of Ethanol Plants

Source: www.ethanolproducer.com/plantmap/2008.

state. For the United States, the number of farms in this category was 485,124. Corn and soybean farms dominate in most of the ten Midwestern states that have been the focus of this analysis. However, the number is somewhat inflated, because other types of farms—those that grow grain and oilseed as well as some dry bean and peas—are also located in these states. The author has adjusted the number downward by 15 percent to account for those other farms, bringing the operative total to 412,355—still significantly higher than the corn- or soybean-farm numbers in the 2002 Census. For the ten Midwestern states, the estimate is 272,338, which is the aggregated Census number less 15 percent. (See Figure 6.5 for state-by-state data.)

Other figures are important here: the number of large corn and soybean farms in these Midwestern states; and the

States	No. of grain, oilseeds, dry bean and dry pea farms[1]	Estimated number of corn, soybean farms (85%)	No. of USDA payment recipients 1995–2006[2]	No. of payment recipients getting 80% of USDA subsidies[3]	Estimated no. of large corn, soybean farms (25%)[4]
1. Iowa	55,294	47,000	177,657	35,531	11,750
2. Nebraska	28,070	23,860	118,945	23,789	5,965
3. Illinois	45,989	39,091	213,520	42,704	9,773
4. Minnesota	36,628	31,134	105,748	21,149	7,783
5. Indiana	28,463	24,194	117,500	23,500	6,048
Top 5 States	194,444	165,277	733,370	146,673	41,319
6. South Dakota	14,792	12,573	64,134	12,826	3,143
7. Ohio	30,873	26,242	99,465	19,893	6,561
8. Kansas	30,326	25,777	168,529	33,705	6,444
9. Wisconsin	25,170	21,395	92,190	18,438	5,349
10. Missouri	24,793	21,074	114,797	22,959	5,269
Next 5 States	125,954	107,061	539,115	107,821	26,765
Top 10 States	320,398	272,338	1,272,485	254,494	68,085
Bottom 40 States	164,726	140,017	N/A	N/A	N/A
Total U.S.[4]	485,124	412,355	N/A	N/A	N/A

Figure 6.5 Estimated Total Number of Corn and Soybean Farms in Top Ten Producing States

Sources: [1]DoA, 2002 Agriculture Census, Number of grains, oilseeds, dry beans, dry pea farms.
[2]EWG website, Farm Subsidy Database, Commodity Subsidies by State 1995–2006, 12-9-08, www.ewg.org/farmsubsidies.
[3]For the Top 10 States, except for Missouri, corn soybean subsidy payments accounted for over 95 percent of payments to the top 20 percent of payment recipients.
[4]Based on the high concentration of large dollar payments to a relatively small number of payment recipients a relatively small number of large farms are clearly inherent in the payment recipient data. The 25 percent is based on that data.

percentage of each state's total production of the two commodities those farms account for. The reason is that large farms receive a huge portion of the DoA subsidy payments for corn and soybeans; the acreage in eligible cropland forms the basis for such payments, and the large farms have the most acreage.

The DoA does not publish those numbers. But the author developed an estimate using DoA subsidy payment data available on the EWG website, www.ewg.org. The site offers an extensive array of data on the departmental subsidies given to "payment recipients" from 1995 to 2006. Payment recipients are entities (individuals, trusts, et al.) that DoA legally recognized as having an ownership interest in a farm that is eligible to receive payments. The latter are based on such criteria as the presence of eligible crops, e.g., corn and soybeans) eligible production acreage, crop yields, and subsidy rates. The DoA uses these variables to determine the amount of subsidy paid each to each recipient.

The EWG site has summarized information on how much of the total corn and soybean subsidies go to the principal recipients of payments. Often, though not always, these recipients are affiliated with the larger farms. The EWG payment-concentration data show that, from 1995 to 2006, the 20 percent of recipients with the largest payments account for 80 percent or more of total DoA corn- and soybean-subsidy payments made in each of the ten states. (See Figure 6.5, columns 4-6.)

Of the 1,017,991 payment recipients in the ten states, 254,494 got on average 84.6 percent of all payment dollars during those years. Using these data, the author assumed that large farms equated to 25 percent of all farms—an estimated 68,085. Farms in these states accounted for 81.7 percent of total U.S. corn production—10.8 billion bushels in 2007. (See Figure 6.6.) The farms in the top five states produced 63.3 percent—8.3 billion bushels. Iowa alone accounted for 18.3 percent of total U.S. corn production and 14.8 percent of soybean production, and has 25.9 percent of U.S. ethanol production capacity. Iowa has clearly hit the corn/soybean/ethanol jackpot.

The other 40 states together account for just 18.3 percent of corn production and only 13.7 percent of ethanol production capacity. That is less than Nebraska alone.

The production of corn in the ten states is closely aligned with its sister crop, soybeans. Historically, most Midwest corn producers have rotated their corn crop with that of soybeans, because the latter restore some of the nitrogen that corn drains from the soil (corn requires substantial amounts of costly nitrogen fertilizer), and soybeans are less water intensive. Most corn farmers do the rotating every second or third year, depending on prices, yields, and conditions. Soybeans are therefore important to corn producers. The same ten states produced 81.5 percent of the total soybean crop in 2007. (See Figures 6.3 and 6.6 for the concentration of soybean production in these states.)

The beneficiaries of the federal ethanol policies are highly concentrated in these ten states, and just five of them account for over 50 percent of the corn, soybean, and ethanol production. Farms in the other 40 states have a small share

States	2008 Ethanol Production Capacity[2]		2007 Corn Production[3]		2007 Soybean Production	
	Billions Gallons (Nr. tenth)	% of US Capacity	Billions Bushels (Nr. tenth)	% of US Production	Billions Bushels (Nr. tenth)	% of US Production
1. Iowa	3.6	25.9	2.4	18.3	0.4	14.8
2. Nebraska	2.0	14.4	1.5	11.5	0.2	7.4
3. Illinois	1.1	7.9	2.3	17.6	0.4	14.8
4. Minnesota	1.1	7.9	1.1	8.4	0.3	11.1
5. Indiana	1.0	7.2	1.0	7.6	0.2	7.4
Top 5 States	8.8	63.3%	8.3	63.4%	1.5	55.6%
6. South Dakota	1.0	7.2	0.5	3.8	0.1	3.7
7. Ohio	0.5	3.6	0.5	3.8	0.2	7.4
8. Kansas	0.5	3.6	0.5	3.8	0.1	3.7
9. Wisconsin	0.4	2.9	0.4	3.1	0.1	3.7
10. Missouri (Corn)[1]	0.4	2.9	0.5	3.8	0.2	7.4
10. North Dakota (Ethanol)[1]	0.4	2.9	0.0	0.0	0.0	0.0
Next 5 States	3.2	23.0%	2.4	18.3%	0.7	25.9%
Top 10 States	12.0	86.3%	10.7	81.7%	2.2	81.5%
Next 40 States	1.9	13.7%	2.4	18.3%	0.5	18.5%
50 State Total	13.9	100.0%	13.1	100.0%	2.7	100.0%

Figure 6.6 Concentrations of Corn, Ethanol, and Soybean Production in Ten Midwestern States

Sources: [1]For the 10th-state rank, Missouri is tenth for corn and North Dakota is tenth for ethanol.
[2]Ethanol Producer, Fall 2008, plants completed and under construction, Fuel Ethanol Plant Map.
[3]DoA/NASS, "Quick Stats," December 2008.

of both the production and the benefits. Overall, an estimated 272,000 farms in the ten states reap the lion's share of from the federal ethanol policy's windfall benefits.

What's the Cost to Consumers and Taxpayers?

An earlier part of this section showed that two to three hundred million or so food and gasoline purchasers, and federal taxpayers pay for the federal ethanol-policy benefits that corn, soybean, and ethanol producers/owners receive. Their payments take two forms. The first is for federal taxes that fund the DoA subsidies, the federal tax credit for ethanol blended into gasoline, and the many other federal subsidies for ethanol.

The second form of payment has several parts, none of which are readily apparent to those who pay. One form is higher food prices caused by the increased demand for corn for fuel ethanol.[60] Another is higher gasoline costs to travel the same number of miles because ethanol-blended gasoline results in less fuel economy. Another is higher prices for ethanol that result from the fee on imports. Yet another is an increase in new car and light-truck vehicle costs because of the need to upgrade fuel systems to burn E10 or higher mixtures. And yet others include the increase in maintenance costs for older boats (outboard motors not able to readily use ethanol-blended gasoline); carbureted motorcycles and small gasoline-engine malfunctions caused by ethanol blended gasoline; and any new-vehicle recalls by manufacturers for problems traceable to the same cause.[61]

Federal subsidy payments (summarized in Figure 6.7) are estimated at $143 billion from 2008–2017. More than 90 percent of them go to DoA payments to corn and soybean producers, and for the ethanol tax credit. The tax credit of 45 cents per gallon for blending ethanol into gasoline is claimed by the blender, but the subsidy increases the price of ethanol received by the ethanol producer. Depending on gasoline and ethanol-market conditions, some of the value of the credit may be captured by refiners and importers. However, the credit was enacted because of the insistence of the ethanol advocates, and that is the main reason the author gives the cost as shown.

Other major subsidy costs include: (1) the deeply subsidized crop insurance available to corn and soybean producers; and (2) a strategic ethanol reserve that could eventually be necessary to deal with corn production shortfalls resulting from Midwestern floods and droughts. On average since 1970, as noted above, one of those has occurred every six or seven years, resulting in a 20- to 30-percent decline in corn production compared to the previous year, according to the DoA. The cost of a 3 billion-gallon reserve has been included at $10 billion for ethanol, storage tanks, and related initial costs based on a DoA/DoE study.[62]

Estimated consumer cost increases for the period 2008–2017 amount to a whopping $363.7 billion, or some $36 billion annually. Consumers seldom miss a few dollars taken from their pockets when the expenditure is not directly tied to ethanol blended gasoline. For example, a consumer who got

[All $ in current $ (not adjusted for inflation) to nearest tenth billion]

	2008–2017

Federal Budget-Cost Increases

- Departments of Agriculture and Energy plus the Environmental Protection Agency

—Various production-related subsidies paid to corn and soybean producers.[1]	$36.4
—Subsidized crop insurance.[1]	30.6
—Disaster payments to corn and soybean producers.[2]	7.2
—Estimated costs of a strategic ethanol reserve of 3 billion gallons to mitigate corn production shortfalls due to floods and droughts.	10.0
—Other federal ethanol-related programs.[3]	N/A

- Department of Treasury

—Tax revenues forgone because of the tax credit for ethanol blending in gasoline.	58.8
—Tax revenues forgone for other ethanol tax subsidies.[4]	N/A
Total estimated federal taxpayer costs:	$143.0

Consumer Cost Increases

• Mileage penalty–lower BTU ethanol blend.	$115.0
• Increase in food costs.[5]	198.1
• Increase in domestic ethanol price resulting from fee on imported ethanol.[6]	35.2
• Increase in vehicle costs for flexible-fuel vehicle upgrade.[7]	15.4
Total estimated consumer costs:	$363.7
Grand total of taxpayer and consumer costs:	$506.7

Figure 6.7 Estimated Impact of Federal Corn-Ethanol Policy on Consumer and Federal Taxpayer Costs, 2008–2017

(continued)

Figure 6.7 *(continued)*

Sources:

[1]CBO's 2008 Summer Baseline budget estimates.

[2]According to the EWG, disaster payments to farmers between 1995 and 2006 averaged 10.8 percent of all commodity-subsidy payments. (See www.ewg.org.) The figure was used for the author's 2008–2017 estimates.

[3]Other programs include the one involving alternative fuel-capable vehicle purchase, purchase of E10, and research and development ethanol-related programs, RFS administrative costs, grants, loans for various ethanol-related purposes, subsidized Rural Utility Service loans for electric generation and transmission in Midwestern states, rural development assistance for ethanol plant siting, and related community development.

[4]Other ethanol tax subsidies including a tax credit for installing E85 gasoline pumps of $30,000 per pump tax credit, a small ethanol producer tax credit.

[5]This is based on the estimated increase in corn, soybean, and wheat prices—using DoA/Economic Research Service (ERS) and NASS data—for those commodities' historic average prices from 1997 to 2005 versus their long-term higher prices from 2008/9 through 2017–2018. Source: DoA long-term price projections, February 2008.

[6]The import fee of 54 cents on U.S. ethanol imports increases domestic ethanol prices. The amount of the increase is paid by ethanol/gasoline consumers. Based on research by Elobeid and Tokgoz published in the *American Journal of Agricultural Economics* entitled "Removing Distortions in the U.S. Ethanol Market: What Does It Imply for the U.S. and Brazil?" November 2008, the estimated amount of price increase is 13.6% or 27 cents per gallon based on an ethanol mandate of 7.5 billion gallons. A higher mandate would increase the value. The 27 cents was used for the estimate of $35.2 billion.

[7]Most manufacturers have committed to producing flexible-fuel vehicles for the bulk of their U.S. sales within a few years. When E10 is increased to E15 and E20, as required under the RFS mandate, flexible-fuel vehicles will be necessary to prevent rust and other problems that foul the fuel system. To cover these costs, an average expenses $150 per vehicle was used.

300 miles from a 15 gallon tank of gasoline prior to E10 now gets about 290 miles. Since most drivers do not check their gas mileage, they are unaware of this stealth ethanol tax, which, when gasoline is $4 per gallon, equals about roughly $75 per year per vehicle. Even drivers who check mileage find it difficult to determine why they're getting fewer miles per tank.

Similarly, consumers cannot discern the increase in food prices caused in part by ethanol. The same is true with the federal taxes paid to cover the substantial ethanol subsidies. But the owners of older boats in California, where ethanol in gasoline allegedly dissolved the fuel tanks and ruined the engines, claimed they were able to trace the cause to the gasoline. They are suing ExxonMobil and Chevron for putting the ethanol in the gasoline! The companies, of course, were just trying to comply with federal law that requires ethanol blending.[63]

Based on EIA's projections for the period 2008 through 2020, the existing corn ethanol federal policies (mandate, subsidy, tariff) do not result in a decrease in gasoline prices in the U.S. compared to the competitive market policy case projections as some ethanol supporters claim. Projected gasoline prices are about the same for the two policy cases for the forecast period; therefore, there isn't a lower gasoline price benefit to consumers under the existing federal ethanol policies.

Overall, about one-half trillion dollars of increase consumer and taxpayer costs (a conservative estimate) were identified. This does not count the hundreds of millions of dollars paid in taxes to states that provide subsidies for ethanol. See Part III, document C (beginning on page 171) for list. Nor does it count the cost of the very large amount of inefficiently used capital that has been invested in corn ethanol plants—a use of capital that makes this country less competitive in world markets, because it forces the U.S. economy to use more ethanol than is economic in place of petroleum gasoline.

Which States Are the Federal Ethanol-Policy Windfall Winners?

Figure 6.8 includes a breakdown of the subsidy payments for each of the top ten corn-, soybean-, and ethanol-producing

State	USDA Subsidy Payments to Corn, Soybean Producers 2008–2017	Federal Ethanol Tax Subsidy 2008–2017	Total Federal Subsidies 2008–2017
1. Iowa	$14.6	$15.2	$29.8
2. Nebraska	8.8	8.5	17.3
3. Illinois	14.2	4.6	18.8
4. Minnesota	7.6	4.6	12.2
5. Indiana	6.3	4.2	10.5
Top 5 States	$51.5	$37.1	88.6
6. South Dakota	3.2	4.2	7.4
7. Ohio	4.0	2.1	6.1
8. Kansas	3.2	2.1	5.3
9. Wisconsin	2.7	1.7	4.4
10. Missouri (Corn)	4.0	0.0	4.0
10. North Dakota (Ethanol)	0.0	1.7	1.7
Top 6–10 States	$17.1	$11.8	28.9
Top 10 States	$68.6	$48.9	117.5
Total US	$84.2	$58.8	143.0
Top 10 as % Total	81.5%	83.2%	

Figure 6.8 Estimated Federal Subsidies to the Top Ten Corn, Soybean, and Ethanol Producers (in current $ to nearest tenth billion)

Sources: CBO, 2008 Summer Baseline for 2008–2017; state detail based on 2007 corn, soybean production percentages. See Figure 6.6; ethanol tax subsidy based on RFS quantities times .45 per gallon times 2008 state by state percentage shares of ethanol production capacity.

Midwestern states. They are estimated to receive over 80 percent of the federal subsidies, while the top *five* states get an estimated 62.8 percent. Iowa alone accounts for over 21 percent of the total.

In addition, from 1995 to 2006, an all-states total of $95.8 billion in DoA subsidy payments were made to corn and soybean producers.[64] Of that amount, $73 billion went to the top ten producing states.

Other Financial Windfalls for Corn and Soybean Farmers. Those who own and operate the farms in the ten Midwestern states get only about 42 percent of their estimated ethanol benefits from the federal subsidies. Additional billions accrue to them via a major increase in farm income and a substantial increase in farmland market value because of higher prices for corn and other crops, induced by the rise in demand for corn for ethanol. In 2008, 9 billion gallons of ethanol were required under provisions of the RFS for gasoline blending—that is, about 3.3 billion bushels of corn, or about 25 percent of the 2008 production. By 2015, the blend quantity increases to 15 billion gallons requiring 5.5 billion bushels of corn—over 40 percent of 2008 production. This will boost prices for corn and other related crops that compete for the same acreage. It is also likely to also mean further increases in net farm income and farmland value.

The estimated increase in net farm income from 2008 through 2017 for corn and soybean producers is $42.4 billion. The figure is based on Economic Research Service (ERS) net farm-income estimates for the period 2000–2007.[65] (See Figure 6.9 for the state-by-state estimates.)

Increase in Farmland Value. In addition to increased net-farm income, corn and soybean producers who own their farmland (as over 90 percent of them do) and absentee farmland owners have enjoyed a very large windfall in relation to the

State	2000	2001	2002	2003	2004	2005	2006	2007	2000–2003 Average	2004–2007 Average	Increase 2004–2007[1]	Increase 2008–2017	Portion attr. to corn, soybeans[2]
1. Iowa	$2.4	$2.4	$2.0	$2.0	$5.6	$4.0	$3.0	$5.3	$2.2	$4.5	103%	$22.8	$10.6
2. Nebraska	1.4	1.9	0.9	2.7	3.5	2.9	1.9	3.4	1.7	2.9	70%	12.0	3.9
3. Illinois	1.7	1.6	0.8	1.6	3.9	1.6	1.7	3.2	1.4	2.6	82%	11.8	7.8
4. Minnesota	1.4	1.0	0.8	1.7	2.8	3.3	2.5	3.4	1.2	3.0	145%	17.8	6.5
5. Indiana	0.9	1.2	0.5	1.3	2.5	1.6	1.5	2.3	1.0	2.0	103%	10.0	5.2
Top 5 States	$7.8	$8.1	$5.0	$9.3	$18.3	$13.4	$10.6	$17.6	$7.6	$15.0	98%	$74.3	$34.0
6. S. Dakota	1.4	1.3	0.5	1.7	2.1	1.9	0.7	2.3	1.2	1.8	43%	5.3	1.5
7. Ohio	1.4	1.4	0.8	1.2	1.7	1.5	1.4	1.9	1.2	1.6	35%	4.3	1.6
8. Kansas	1.1	1.3	0.4	2.0	2.1	2.4	1.1	2.1	1.2	1.9	60%	7.3	1.1
9. Wisconsin	0.8	1.2	1.0	1.7	1.9	1.7	1.3	2.6	1.2	1.9	60%	7.0	1.1
10. Missouri	1.0	1.1	0.7	1.1	2.6	1.7	1.6	2.0	1.0	2.0	103%	10.0	3.1
Next 5 States	$5.7	$6.3	$3.4	$7.7	$10.4	$9.2	$6.1	$10.9	$5.8	$9.2	58%	$33.8	$8.4
Top 10 States	$13.5	$14.4	$8.4	$17.0	$28.7	$22.6	$16.7	$28.5	$13.3	$24.1	81%	$108.0	$42.4
Total U.S.	$50.6	$54.9	$39.6	$60.5	$85.8	$79.3	$57.6	$86.0	$51.4	$77.2	50%	N/A	N/A
%Top 5	15%	15%	13%	15%	21%	17%	18%	20%	15%	19%			
% Top 10	27%	26%	21%	28%	33%	28%	29%	33%	26%	31%			

Figure 6.9 Estimated U.S. Net Farm Income: Ten States with the Highest Corn and Soybean Production

Notes: [1]The increase is the difference between 2000–2003 and 2004–2007 averages times 10 (years).

[2]The portion of the net income increase attributed to corn, soybeans based on corn, soybean "Value of Crop Production percent share," ERS, 8-28-08.

Source: DoA, Economic Research Service (ERS), "Net Farm Income 1990–2007", 8-12-08.

value of the farm. This increase was largely caused by heightened demand for corn to make fuel ethanol. The ERS publishes average farmland-value data each year by state. This information is a statewide average, calculated on a per-acre basis.

Farmland owners throughout each state benefit because of the substantial number of acres required to produce the corn for ethanol. But in many of these states corn and soybean production takes a large amount of the cropland available. Thus, some of the higher demand will be met by acres diverted from other crops such as wheat, cotton, and rice. Also, corn exports will be diverted to domestic use. With continued and substantial increases in corn demand to meet the ethanol RFS, it is highly likely that farmland values will continue to increase above the levels experienced through 2007.

Multiplying ERS state-by-state farmland values times the number of acres devoted to corn and soybean production in 2007, the increase in farmland value is $98.9 billion. (See Figure 6.10, Column 3.)

Summarized in Figure 6.10 are estimates of the benefits that corn/soybean farms are receiving or will receive from 2008 through 2017. The estimate is $258.8 billion for only the top ten Midwestern states. That represents a huge transfer of wealth, considering the small number of farm beneficiaries involved.

This already-enormous transfer of wealth has no end in sight. It now seems to be a permanent entitlement to the corn and soybean farm owners and operators. Eighty years ago, ironically, the early settlers of these states produced corn with no federal assistance at all (note that some of the

State	Federal Subsidies[1]	Estimated Increase in Net Income 2008-2017[2]	Actual Increase in Farmland Value[3]	Total Estimated Benefits
1. Iowa	$29.8	$10.6	$24.9	$65.3
2. Nebraska	17.3	3.9	5.8	27.0
3. Illinois	18.8	7.8	31.2	57.8
4. Minnesota	12.2	6.5	10.1	28.8
5. Indiana	10.5	5.2	10.7	26.4
Top 5 States	$88.6	$34.0	$82.7	$205.3
6. S. Dakota	7.4	1.5	2.2	11.1
7. Ohio	6.1	1.6	4.4	12.1
8. Kansas	5.3	1.1	1.7	8.1
9. Wisconsin	4.4	1.1	5.1	10.6
10. Missouri	4.0	3.1	2.8	9.9
10. N. Dakota	1.7	0.0	N/A	1.7
Top 6–10 Slates	$28.9	$8.4	$16.2	$53.5
Top 10 States	$117.5	$42.4	$98.9	$258.8
Total U.S.	$143.0	$258.0	?	?
Top 10 states as % of U.S.	82.2%	16.4%		

Figure 6.10 Estimated Total Federal Benefits Provided to Corn, Soybean, and Ethanol Producers in Ten Midwestern States, 2008–2017

Sources: [1]From Figure 6.8.

[2]The increase in income for corn, soybean producers is in major part attributable to the implementation of the RFS that started in 2005. Only the average increase from 2004 to 2007 compared to 2000 to 2003 has been included in the estimates. As the RFS quantity increases from 9.0 billion gallons in 2008 to 15.0 in 2015, it is very likely incomes will increase above the level included. For this reason, the Net Income increase is a low estimate.

[3]DoA/ERS, Average Value Per Acre of Farm Real Estate, January 1, 2000 to January 1, 2008. This is a one-time increase. As the RFS increases from 2008 to 2015, an additional 2.2 billion bushels of corn per year will be needed. At current yields, this requires an additional 15 million acres of farmland or an increase of about 17 percent. Over the long term, this could increase farmland values in major corn farming states beyond 2007 levels.

settlers received free acreage). And it is even more ironic that a few centuries ago, North American natives produced corn without any government subsidy. What an amazing feat that must have been!

How Substantial Are the Federal Benefits on a Per-Farm Basis?

The average benefit for corn and soybean farms in all ten Midwestern states is about $1 million per farm over the ten-year period, or just under $100,000 per year. That is almost precisely double the median U.S. household income.[66] Federal ethanol policy is highly regressive, imposing costs on low- to middle-income households while providing benefits to farms that almost certainly have household incomes well above the median.

The average annual benefit for the top five producing states is $1.2 million per farm—with Iowa at $1.4 million —and nearly $140,000 per farm per year. (See Figure 6.11.) Those averages mask the huge benefits accruing to the *large*-scale corn and soybean farms within these states. For those large farms, the ten-state average is $2.7million, $270,000 per year. Even more blessed are the top five states where the average is $3.9, or about $400,000 per year; in Iowa, it is more than $4.3 million—$430,000-plus annually. These are very substantial windfalls, all the more so for a policy that has no significant energy benefits to the nation but imposes substantial economic costs on its citizens.

State	Total Estimated Federal Benefits (Nearest tenth billion)	Estimated No. Corn, Soybean Farms	Per Farm Average Benefit (Nominal $)	Estimated No. Large Corn, Soybean Farms	Per Average Large Farm Benefit (Nominal $)
1. Iowa	$65.3	47,000	$1,389,362	11,750	$4,334,809
2. Nebraska	27.0	23,860	1,131,601	5,965	3,666,387
3. Illinois	57.8	39,091	1,478,601	9,773	4,967,973
4. Minnesota	28.8	31,134	925,034	7,783	2,960,298
5. Indiana	26.4	24,194	1,091,180	6,048	3,623,016
Top 5 States	$205.3	165,279	$1,242,142	41,319	3,910,497
6. S. Dakota	11.1	12,573	882,844	3,143	2,895,959
7. Ohio	12.1	26,242	461,093	6,561	1,586,039
8. Kansas	8.1	25,777	314,234	6,444	1,081,006
9. Wisconsin	10.6	21,395	495,443	5,349	1,624,977
10. Missouri	9.9	21,074	469,773	5,269	1,634,656
10. N. Dakota	1.7	N/A	N/A	N/A	N/A
Top 6–10 States	$53.5	107,061	$499,715	26,766	$1,548,326
Top 10 States	$258.8	272,340	$950,283	68,085	$2,729,411

Figure 6.11 Federal Corn, Soybean, and Ethanol Benefits, 2008–2017

Source: From Figures 5.1, 6.5.

What Are the Costs Under the Competitive-Market Ethanol Policy?

Throughout this book, a benefit-cost comparison has been made to current ethanol policy versus a policy based on competitive markets. A large body of empirical evidence has proved that a competitive market policy is most efficient and effective. Therefore, when the U.S. government substitutes an interventionist policy, as it has for ethanol, the national benefits should be large and exceed the costs. Is that the case for federal ethanol?

Under a competitive market approach, federal budget costs would decrease substantially—probably by 50 percent —with the elimination of the tax subsidies and (if it were created) the strategic ethanol reserve. Such a reserve would not be needed because about one-fifth of the ethanol consumed in the United States would come from Brazil—from a different crop and weather system, thereby increasing the reliability of ethanol supply. Instead of consuming 15 billion gallons of ethanol per year, the total would be about 10 billion, with some 8 billion from domestic production.[67] Thus a bad weather year in the Midwest would have far less impact and would probably be offset in part by an increase in Brazilian ethanol imports.

Lower prices might produce an increase in DoA subsidies for corn and soybeans, but it is very unlikely that the increase would offset the saving from the elimination of the tax credit. In addition, billions in capital that would have been invested in uneconomic ethanol plants would go instead to investments with a prospect of a financial return, thereby increasing employment and GDP.

Consumer costs would also be far lower than under current ethanol policy, since most ethanol blending would occur in the Midwest. The mileage penalty would be reduced by at least one third and the food-cost increase by one half; the increase in transportation costs would probably decrease substantially, because E7 would be the average blend—not the E12 necessary to comply with the RFS at 15 billion gallons per year in 2014. A considerable portion of the gasoline sold would contain no ethanol. Refiners would meet octane requirements through their traditional method of additional refining steps to increase octane. A large part of the unknown maintenance costs for boat, motorcycle, and auto manufacturers, as well as small-engine owners, would probably disappear as plain, ordinary gasoline—without ethanol —was distributed to most service stations.

A competitive market for gasoline costs far less for taxpayers and consumers. In addition, the windfall to the 272,000 corn and soybean farmers in the ten Midwestern states would be much less (though still significant, considering EIA estimates of the amount of ethanol blended in gasoline each per year).

In sum, current federal-ethanol policy is very costly to taxpayers and consumers, who get few, if any, benefits. Under current policy mandates, a level of 15 billion gallons per year results in only 5.2 billion gallons more ethanol than what EIA says would be the case if a competitive market policy were in place. This incremental 5.2 billion gallons, when adjusted for ethanol's lower BTU content, amounts to just

3.4 billion gallons of gasoline equivalent. In a U.S. gasoline market of nearly 140 billion gallons annually, that amounts to a mere 2 percent. Further, if the 3.4 billion is adjusted downward for the domestic energy consumed to produce the ethanol, the net amount is insignificant.

Current ethanol policy is designed to transfer a large amount of wealth from consumers and taxpayers to corn and soybean farm operators/owners and ethanol producers. The wealth transfer is far greater than would be realized under a competitive market policy. More important, current policy effectively rules out the development of any new fuel or blend that might be superior to corn ethanol. The beneficiaries—that small number of farmers, farm land owners in those ten Midwestern states—are indeed reaping billions in windfalls.

7

Conclusions

....

A fter completing a comprehensive review of the
most important claims made by the advocates for
federal ethanol policy, in this author's view the policy has
little to do with energy and a lot to do with wealth transfer.

Only one of the claims was found to be true: the policy
does create jobs in rural areas, mainly the top ten producing
states. All other claims investigated were found to be questionable or not correct. The evidence used by the responsible
federal agencies (DoE, DoA, the EPA) to justify the policy
was found to be flawed. Even though the policy in its current
form is nearly four years old (dating from the Energy Policy Act of 2005), the agencies continue to use these flawed
claims to support it. The lone exception: the recently published EPA proposed regulation for the Renewable Fuels
Standard.

The facts and reasons supporting the author's conclusion
were presented in Chapters 3 and 4. First and foremost is that
current policy does not, based on EIA's forecast, significantly

increase domestic transportation-fuel supplies over the quantity that would be developed by a competitive market policy. You can get two-thirds the level of ethanol use in the United States without a RFS mandate, a 45 cent-per-gallon tax subsidy, corn and soybean subsidies, and an import fee on ethanol imports.

Second, current policy already has made, and will con-tinue to make, massive wealth transfers from federal taxpay-ers, gasoline consumers, and food consumers to corn and soybean farmers and ethanol producers. Over $500 billion dollars in costs, it is estimated, have been or will be incurred from 2008 to 2017. The primary beneficiaries are the owners and/or operators of an estimated 270,000 corn and soybean farms located in ten Midwestern states.

Third, the large corn/soybean farms, farmers in these states reap the majority of the benefits. Large farm owners and operators in Iowa, for example, took in or will take in on average an estimated $4.3 million from 2008 to 2017.

Fourth, there is no end game for the policy. Even after thirty years of ethanol subsidies (more than seventy years for corn), the wealth transfer continues year in and year out. The policy gives every appearance of being permanent, despite the fact that it has never—and will never—produce the claimed benefits except for the increases in rural employment.

Fifth, a 2009 CBO report concluded: "It is unlikely that, on average, over the past several decades ethanol produc-ers would have turned a profit if they had not received pro-duction subsidies."[68] That conclusion is compelling, if not startling, because after three decades of federal subsidies, ethanol remains uneconomic—even with the subsidies—as evidenced by the spate of ethanol-related bankruptcies and plant shutdowns in the past year.

Sixth, the safety hazards and costs of transporting the billions of gallons of ethanol produced in the Midwest to the east, gulf and west coasts mainly by rail are of major concern. Rail accidents involving ethanol tank car derailments, explosions and fires are inevitable. An event in Illinois involved tank cars of ethanol exploding and bursting into flames, killing one person and injuring several others.[69]

Finally, under current federal ethanol policy the estimated federal budget cost for each incremental gallon of ethanol produced (on a petroleum equivalent basis) compared to a competitive market policy is $5.91 per gallon or $248.22 per barrel. At this rate to reduce U.S. petroleum imports by two million barrels per day or about 20 percent would cost over $181 billion annually just in taxpayer subsidies. Clearly, reducing petroleum imports with the current ethanol policy is a costly ineffective policy.

The nation and its taxpayers and consumers would be far better off if the federal government adopted a competitive market-reliance policy for ethanol and thereby avoided the very substantial costs that current ethanol policy has imposed on the nation's consumers and taxpayers. The currrent corn ethanol policies should be phased out over a year or two.

A

International Energy Agency, IEA Response System for Oil Supply Emergencies

(For a detailed description of the system, go to http://www.iea.org/publications/free_new_Desc.asp?PUBS_ID=1912)

The IEA was established in 1974 in response to the oil supply interruption of 1973. Currently it has twenty-eight industrialized member countries (nearly all rely on imported oil) that are committed to having oil available and taking joint measures to deal with the adverse impacts of oil supply interruptions. The member countries' IEA strategy is to be prepared in advance to take collective action in the event of an interruption. The member countries believe that the adverse consequences of an interruption can be mitigated more effectively on a collective basis than by one country acting alone.

The IEA was established by a treaty agreement signed by all twenty-eight member countries. The IEA is an autonomous agency funded by its member countries and linked to the Organization for Economic Co-operation and Development (OECD). The IEA has a full-time staff and its member countries meet regularly.

The twenty-eight IEA member countries include Australia, Austria, Belgium, Canada, Czech Republic, Denmark, Finland, France, Germany, Greece, Hungary, Ireland, Italy, Japan, Korea (Republic of), Luxembourg, Netherlands, New Zealand, Norway, Poland, Portugal, Slovak Republic, Spain, Sweden, Switzerland, Turkey, United States, and United Kingdom.

An emergency response to an oil supply interruption is the IEA's primary mission. Response measures include member countries being required to hold oil stocks equivalent to ninety days of net imports; in the event of a major oil supply disruption, the member would release the stocks, restrain demand, switch to other fuels, increase domestic production (or share available stocks if necessary), and share oil market and other information. Coordination and dialogue would ensue with other consuming countries that are not members of the IEA.

In addition, an international energy forum has been established to provide a framework for a continuing dialogue between energy-producing and energy-consuming countries. Eighty-seven country ministers, representing countries that account for 90 percent of global oil and gas supply and demand, have signed the charter. The IEF charter calls for the creation of transparent and stable global oil and gas markets.

For more information on the IEA, go to www.iea.org

B
History of World Oil Market Petroleum-supply Interruptions

INTERAGENCY WORKING GROUP

Strategic Petroleum Reserve
Analysis of Size Options

February 1990

U.S. Department of Energy
Washington, DC 20585

Acknowledgement

This interagency study was chaired by the Department of Energy,
with the participation of the following agencies:

The Department of State
The Department of the Treasury
The Department of Defense
The Department of the Interior
The Department of Commerce
The Office of Management and Budget
The Central Intelligence Agency
The National Security Council
The Economic Policy Council
The Council of Economic Advisers
The Federal Emergency Management Agency
The Energy Information Administration

Table 4-1
PAST DISRUPTIONS OF OIL PRODUCTION
PERCENT CHANGE IN WORLD OIL PRICES

Dates		Duration (in Months)	Magnitude Of Supply Shortfall (Million b/d)	Percent Change in World Oil Prices (US$/barrel)
March 1951–October 1954	Iranian Fields Nationalized. Iranian oilfields were nationalized on May I, following two months of unrest and strikes in the Abadan area. Major oil companies boycotted Iranian oil on the world oil market and instituted court actlons to deter potential buyers.	44	0.7	+12.9 (1.71 to 1.93)
November 1956–March 1951	Suez War. Nasser closed the Suez Canal in the wake of the Anglo-French–Israeli incursion. At the same time, the Iraqi Petroleum Company (IPC) pipeline was damaged in Syri a, and Saudi Arabia embargoed oil shipments to the United Kingdom and France.	4	2.0	–1.6 (1.93 to 1.90)
December 1966–March 1967	Syrian Transit Fee Dispute. Syria imposed new transit taxes on the IPC pipelines to the Mediterranean. IPC stopped the flow of oil. refusing to pay the higher taxes. Iraq demanded full revenues from the oil companies operating there, despite the diminished production.	3	0.7	No Change (1.35)
June 1967–August 1967	Six Day War. Suez Canal closed. and IPC and Tapline pipelines shut down following the Israeli strike into the Sinai. Oil exports were embargoed to Western Europe—particularly to the United Kingdom, West Germany and the United States.	2	2.0	No Change (1.35)
July 1967–October 1968	Nigerian Civil War. Oil terminals were blockaded hy the Nigerian Federal Navy, blocking off exports. Shell and BP ceased production in the country during most of the war.	35	0.5	–3.7 (1.35 to 1.30)
May 1970–January 1971	Libyan Price Controversy. Libya gradually reduced the authorized production by selected oil companies, claiming potential damage to the oilfields. At the same time. the Tapline was damaged in Syria, forcing a shutdown until Syria authorized repairs. Production cuts were restored, and the pipeline in Syria was quickly repaired once Libya obtained higher oil prices from the companies.	9	1.3	≈25 (1.94 to 2.42)

Dates		Duration (in Months)	Magnitude Of Supply Shortfall (Million b/d)	Percent Change in World Oil Prices (US$/barrel)
April 1971– August 1971	Algerian-French Nationalization Struggle. Algeria nationalized 51 percent of the oil companies and pipelines—all French owned— operating within its borders and announced compensation plans. The Algerians then unilaterally raised oil export prices to French firms, leading the companies to seek a worldwide embargo against Algerian oil. Algeria retaliated by suspending oil deliveries to French tankers. claiming that the companies owed back taxes. Oil flows resumed in August after a CFP-Algerian agreement in July. All other companies accepted the Algerian terms by December.	5	0.6	No Change (1.75)
March 1973– Mary 1973	Lebansese Political Conflict. Unrest in Lebanon disrupted the flow of oil from Iraq and Saudi Arabia. Following a Lebanese takeover ot IPC facilities near Tripoli, Iraq cut off oil exports to Lebanon and was denied use of Lebanon's transit facilities. In April, a storage tank and parts of the Tapline facility at Sidon were destroyed by sabotage.	2	0.5	+26 (2.30 to 2.90)
October 1973– March 1974	The October Arab-Israeli War. CAPEC embargoed oil shipments to selected western countries and reduced oil production. Transit through the Suez Canal was halted, further delaying shipments to the United States and Western Europe. OPEC production returned to the level of October 1973 in the first quarter of 1974. Saudi Arabia finally ended the embargo on 18 March 1974.	5	1.6	+276 (3.00 to 11.34)
April 1976– May 1976	Civil War in Lebanon. Political instability in Lebanon led Iraq to reduce oil exports via the pipelines through Lebanon to the Mediterranean.	2	0.3	No Change (11.50)
May 1977	Damage at a Saudi Oilfield. Fires damaged a gas-oil separation facility at Saudi Arabia's Abgaig field. Repairs took nearly one year, but other Saudi production quickly offset the loss.	1	0.7	No Change (12.70)

Dates		Duration (in Months)	Magnitude Of Supply Shortfall (Million b/d)	Percent Change in World Oil Prices (US$/barrel)
November 1978–23.55) April 1979	Iranian Revolution. Unrest in the oilfields shut down production during the fourth quarter of 1978 and the first quarter of 1979. Output was gradually restored to around 4 million b/d starting in May 1979.	6	3.7	+82.4 (12.91 to
October 1980–january 1981	Outbreak of Iran-Iraq war. The Iraqi-initiated regional conflict sharply curtailed oil exports from both countries, particularly through the Persian Gulf. There were intermittent air attacks and sabotage damage to export terminals, processing facilities, and pipelines in both countries.	3	3.0	+9.8 (31.74 to 34.84)
July 1988–17.78) August 1988	UK North Sea Piper Alpha Platform Explosion. A gas explosion completely destroyed the Piper Platform, killing 167 people while stopping exports of over 300,000 b/d from the Flotta onshore terminal. Reconstruction of the Piper platform is not expected until 1992. Production ot about 35,000 b/d from surrounding platforms has been successfully restored.	2	0.3	+23.4 (14.41 to
December 1988–March 1989	UK North Sea Fulmer Floating Storage Accident. The Fulmer floating storage vessel broke away from its moorings damaging the export facilities there and halting oil flow. Temporary repairs restored 100,000 b/d in March 1989.	4	0.2	+7.9 (16.13 to 17.40)
April 1989–17.48) June 1989	UK North Sea Cormorant Central Platform Explosion. A gas leak and explosion at the key UK North Sea Cormorant Central platform stopped production of over 500,000 b/d. Partial production resumed in June 1989.	2	0.5	−17.48 (18.99 to

Table 4-2

WORLD OIL SUPPLY DISRUPTIONS
PERCENT OF WORLD OIL CONSUMPTION
1951–1989

Dates	Supply Disruption	Magnitude of Supply Shortfall (mmb/d)	World Oil Consumption (mmb/d)	Percent of Consumption
March 1951–October 1954	Iranian Fields Nationalized	0.7	13.22	5.30
November 1956–March 1957	Suez War	2.0	17.5	11.43
December 1966–March 1967	Syrian Transit Fee Dispute	0.7	34.3	2.04
June 1967–August 1967	Six Day War	2.0	40.0	5.00
July 1967–October 1968	Nigerian Civil War	0.5	40.1	1.25
May 1970–January 1971	Libyan Price Controversy	1.3	48.0	2.71
April 1971–August 1971	Algerian-French Nationalization Struggle	0.6	50.2	1.20
March 1973–May 1973	Lebanese Political Conflict	0.5	58.2	0.86
October 1973–March 1974	October Arab-Israeli War	1.6	58.2	2.75
April 1976–May 1976	Civil War in Lebanon	0.3	60.2	0.50
May 1977	Damage at Saudi Oilfield	0.7	62.1	1.13
November 1978–April 1979	Iranian Revolution	3.7	65.1	5.68
October 1980–January 1981	Outbreak of Iran-Iraq War	3.0	60.4	4.97
July 1988–November 1989	UK Piper Alpha Offshore Platform Explosion	0.3	49.8	0.60
December 1988–March 1989	UK Fulmer Floating Storage Vessel Accident	0.2	51.6	0.39
April 1989–June 1989	UK Cormorant Offshore Platform	0.5	51.6	0.97

(

State-by-State Ethanol Subsidies

Biofuels – At What Cost?
Government support for ethanol and biodiesel in the United States

One of a series of reports addressing subsidies for biofuels in
Australia, Brazil, Canada, the European Union,
Switzerland and the United States.

www.globalsubsidies.org

October 2006

Prepared by:
Doug Koplow, Earth Track, Inc.
Cambridge, MA

Prepared for:
The Global Subsidies Initiative (GSI)
of the International Institute for Sustainable Development (IISD)
Geneva, Switzerland

  | **GSI** Global Subsidies Initiatives

 **iisd** International Institute for Sustainable Development / Institut international du développement durable

 **earth track** www.earthtrack.net

Republished with permission of the International Institute for Sustainable Development (IISD)
www.iisd.org.

Annex

Table A1: Summary of Government Subsidy Programs to Ethanol and Biodiesel

	Subsidy Description	Fuel	Cat	Subsidy Rate ($mils)	Comments/ Other Eligibility Criteria
Producer production incentives (not capped)					
Alaska	E10 reduction supposedly limited in practice to Anchorage during the winter. As of 2004, there was also a 60 month tax credit for E10 produced from wood or wood waste (CEC, 23), or seafood waste.				
Arkansas	Supplier tax refund for biodiesel blends. Rate of $1/gal for B2 or higher; $0.50/gal for B1 (Biodiesel Mag., see source col.). Must have capacity of 1 million gallons within 12 month period (EERE, May 2006).	Biodiesel	Producer		Minimum capacity of 1 mmgy; max blend of B2.
California	40 cpg production incentive for liquid fuels fermented in this state from biomass and biomass-derived resources produced in this state. Eligible liquid fuels include, but are not limited to, ethanol, methanol, and vegetable oils. Eligible biomass resources include, but are not limited to, agricultural products and byproducts, forestry products and byproducts, and industrial wastes (CA Public Resources Code 25678).	Both	Producer	Never funded. (MacDonald, 13 June 2006).	From CA Clean Fuels Act.
Florida	County waste credits for diversion of yard wastes into a range of beneficial reuse, including ethanol production. Likely an indirect and minor effect on ethanol production within the state (EERE, May 2006).	Ethanol	Producer		
Indiana	Biodiesel Blending tax credit of 2 cpg of blended biodiesel (EERE, May 2006). If blend is B2, this is equivalent to $1/gallon of blending oil. This appears to be in addition to the biodiesel PTC.	B2 and higher, but excluding B100.	Producer	Lifetime limit of $3m per facility.	Both the biodiesel blend and the biodiesel used in the blend, must be produced at a facility located inside of Indiana. Advanced approval from the Indiana Economic Development Corporation is required (EERE, May 2006). [Are these types of restrictions constitutional?] Spending on all 3 IN producer subsidies capped at $50m for all taxable years after 31 December 2004.
Indiana	Biodiesel PTC of $1/gallon blended to at least B2. Incentive must be applied for with the Indiana Economic Development Corporation. (IN Code 6-3.1-27).	Biodiesel	Producer	Lifetime limit of $3m per facility, or $5m with special state approval.	Only biodiesel produced within Indiana is eligible. Total program cost for this, the IN ethanol PTC, and the IN biodiesel blending credit is capped at $50m.
Indiana	Biodiesel retailer tax credit of 1 cpg of blended biodiesel distributed by the taxpayer for retail purposes (EERE, May 2006). At B2, this would be equivalent to 50 cpg of blending oil.	Biodiesel	Producer	Lifetime limit of $1m for all retailers in the state.	This is not subject to the state-wide $50m cap.

	Subsidy Description	Fuel	Cat	Subsidy Rate ($mils)	Comments/ Other Eligibility Criteria
Iowa	PTC of 3 cpg to fuel distributors selling B2 so long as 50% or more of the distributors' sales are B2 or higher blends (Pearson, 30 May 2006).	B2 and higher		IA sold 75 million gallons of biodiesel in 2005 (Lincoln Energy, p. 4)	Signed into law 5/30/06. HF 2754 and HF 2759.
Iowa	Retail tax credit of 25 cpg for E85 (HF2754 and appropriation HF2759). Iowa sold 600,000 gallons of E85 in 2005; this provides a floor to calculate the E85 tax credit for 2006. Stats from Lincoln Energy (p. 3): http://www.lincolnway energy.com/newsletter/january_06.pdf	E85			Retroactive to 1 January 2006.
Iowa	Incremental tax credit of 2.5 cpg for retailers for whom >60% of total gallons sold contain some blended ethanol. Runs from 2002–2007 (ACE, 16). Gallons up to 60% do not get the credit. Estimate assumes equal sales per retailer, with 40% of total volume getting the credit.	Ethanol		State has poor tracking systems for tax credits. See Schuling, IA Dept. of Revenue, December 2005.	The Iowa corn growers association notes that 75% of gas sold in IA in 2005 was 10% ethanol or higher. Reasonable to assume that nearly all contained some blended ethanol, and received the tax credit. 1.211 billion gallons of ethanol-blended fuel were sold in Iowa in 2005 (IA Corn).
Maine	5 cpg PTC for ethanol and biodiesel, starting 1 January 2004. Substitution for any liquid fuel is eligible (EERE, May 2006).	Both	Producer	As of mid-2006, ME had no ethanol plants and one pending biodiesel plant at 300,000 gpy.	
Montana	Distributor tax rebate of 2 cpg of biodiesel sold (equivalent to $1/gal of B100) if biodiesel sourced entirely from MT feedstocks (EERE, May 2006; MT Code 15-70-369).	Biodiesel			
Nebraska	Floor Stocks Tax on Ethanol and Biodiesel. A floor stocks tax is an excise tax levied on inventoried fuel. In 2004, Nebraska shifted the point of tax levy from blending to when the fuel is received. As a result, there was an existing inventory of fuel that would have escaped all taxation without the floor stocks tax. This levy applies only to the transitional inventory, and does not represent any incremental tax burden on either fuel (NE DOR, 2004; NE Statute 66-4, 146.01).	Ethanol, biodiesel	Production	Not applicable.	
North Dakota	Biodiesel income tax credit, to blenders, of 5 cpg of diesel fuel B5 or higher. This translates to $1 per gallon of biologically-derived oil.	B5 or higher.			
Ohio	Producer payment up to 50% of invested capital; expires tax year 2013 (F.O. Licht).	Ethanol			
Government renewable-fuel vehicle purchase mandates					
Colorado	State fleet purchase mandate for B20 by 1 January 2007; when available, and at price premiums of less than 10% (NBB, 25 May 2006).	Biodiesel	Purchase preference		
Indiana	Biodiesel Price preference allows government entities to purchase B20 or above for fleet use even at a 10% price premium over standard gas and diesel (EERE, May 2006).	Biodiesel			

Subsidy Description	Fuel	Cat	Subsidy Rate ($mils)	Comments/ Other Eligibility Criteria
Producer production incentives (capped)				
Federal	EPACT 942 production incentives for cellulosic biofuels, to deliver the first billion gallons by 2015. Annual auctions of 100 mmgy of capacity, with incentive going to lowest requested subsidy per gallon delivered. Winning bid gets subsidy for 6 years (EPACT 942).	Ethanol		Initial authorization: $250m.	Limits: No more than $100m/year; $1 billion for entire provision. Single project may not receive more than 25% of total annual subsidy paid out. Interesting policy design.
Arkansas	Production linked grants – at discretion of Ark. Alternative Fuels Commission (EERE, May 2006).	Biodiesel	Producer		Not guaranteed; rates of up to 10 cpg; max. of 5 mgpy per producer; max. duration of grants is 5 yrs.
Arkansas	50 cpg excise tax credit on B100 gallons used for blending (Pearson, 30 May 2006).	Biodiesel	Producer		Limited to the first 2 per cent of total gallons of biodiesel blended.
Hawaii	Producer tax credits of 30 cpg for facilities entering production prior to 01.01.2012 and with at least 75% capacity utilization. Facility size limits. Total credits per plant for maximum of 10 years or $4.5 million. Total annual credits for state capped at first 40 mmgy (or $12m/year) (ACE, 12; HI Revised Statutes, 235-110.3).				Eligible for plants between 0.5 and 15 mmgy in capacity. Max. annual credit = 30% of nameplate capacity (EERE, May 2006). At minimum production of 75% of nameplate required for eligibility, the per gallon tax credit would be 40 cpg of ethanol. Once state capacity >40 mmgy, no new plants will be certified to receive credits (HI statutes).
Illinois	Renewable Fuels Development Program provides producer subsidies for new biofuels production facilities in IL. Rate is 10 cpg for new facilities or 5 cpg for modifying or retrofitting old ones, with a maximum grant of $6.5 million. IL Public Act 93-15 (IL DCEO, RFDP, 2006).	Both	Grant	$15m in 2004; $20m in 2007 (IL Farm Bureau, 2006).	Facility must have annual production capacity of at least 30 mmgy, and grant must be <10% of the total construction costs of the facility.
Indiana	Production tax credit of 12.5 cpg of ethanol for plants that built or increased capacity by 40 mmgy subsequent to 12.31.03. (IN Code 6-3.1-28)	Ethanol	Producer	Lifetime cap of $2m for plants 40-60 mmgy; $3m if >60 mmgy capacity.	3 plants now under construction: 2 @ 40 mmgy; 1 @ 100 mmgy. Lifetime caps mean these plants will max out PTC in their first year of production.
Kansas	Kansas Qualified Biodiesel Producer Incentive Fund provides production tax credit of 30 cpg to qualified biodiesel fuel producers. (NBB, 25 May 2006).	Biodiesel	Producer	3.5000	Effective for sales beginning 1 April 2007. Total funding for the incentive program appears to be $3.5m/year.

	Subsidy Description	Fuel	Cat	Subsidy Rate ($mils)	Comments/ Other Eligibility Criteria
Kansas	PTC of 5 cpg of ethanol produced from capacity predating 07.01.2001, running from 2002–05. New capacity >5 MGY can earn credits of 7.5 cpg on up to 10 MGY ($750k/plant). Capacity expansions of older plants of at least 5 MGY can also earn 7.5 cpg credit, up to 15 MGY new capacity ($1.125m/plant) (ACE, 17). Credits in 2001–2004 were 5 cpg (EERE, May 2006).				
Kentucky	Biodiesel income tax credit of $1 per gallon, available to producers or blenders. Program cap of $1.5 million per year (EERE, May 2006).	Biodiesel	Producer	1.5m/year.	
Maryland	Ethanol PTC of 20 cpg for ethanol produced from small grains; 5 cpg for other agricultural feedstocks such as corn. Maximum of 15 mmgy eligible for the tax credit, of which at least 10 mmgy must be from small grains. (EERE, May 2006).	Ethanol	Producer	Max. value of $0.20 x 10 mmgy + $0.05 x 5 mmgy, or 2.25m/year.	
Maryland	Biodiesel PTC of 20 cpg if from soybean oil produced at a facility built or expanded after 12.31.2004. PTC of 5 cpg if from another feedstock, or from soy in a plant built prior to 12.31.2004. Annual cap of 2 mmgy from new soy capacity and 3 mmgy from other capacity (EERE, May 2006).	Biodiesel	Producer	Max. value of $0.20 x 2 mmgy + $.05 x 3 mmgy, or 350k/year.	
Minnesota	Blender's Tax credit. Between 1980 and 1997, E10 or higher paid 4 cpg less than gasoline in excise taxes (Rankin, 2002).	E10 or higher	Producer	The MN Taxpayers League estimates total payments during this period at $208m (2006$). Heimdahl, June 2006).	
Minnesota	PTC of 20 cpy (13 cpg effective 2003), for a period of 10 years. Annual payments capped at $1.95m per producer (ACE, 24; EERE, May 2006). Multiple plants with a single controlling interest would count as a single producer; minority interests would not (MN Statutes 41A.09). New enrollments ceased in 2004.	Ethanol	Producer	See Text Box 4.1.	Capacity increases subsequent to the initial cut-off date are eligible for the PTC, and for its full 10 years (MN 41A.09, Subd. 3a (c)). Capacity above 15 mmgy does not earn PTCs.
Mississippi	20 cpg PTC for ethanol from production entering the market on or before 30 June 2005. Payments for up to 10 years from point production entered the market; limited to $6m/producer per year; and $37m statewide to all producers in a year (ACE, 25; MS statutes 69-51-5).	Ethanol	Producer		Capacity above 30 mmgy not eligible for PTC.
Missouri	PTC of 20 cpg on first 12.5 MGY of production: and 5 cpg on up to the next 12.5 MGY. Eligibility period applies to first five years of production, expiring 12.31.2005. Capped at $3.125 million over five years (ACE, 26).	Ethanol	Producer		Plants must be located in MO, and 51% of the ownership must be by agricultural producers engaged commercially in farming (MO Revised Statutes, 142.028, 142.029).

	Subsidy Description	Fuel	Cat	Subsidy Rate ($mils)	Comments/ Other Eligibility Criteria
Missouri	Qualified Biodiesel Producer Incentive Fund provides a monthly grant to producers of 30 cpg for the first 15 mmgy of B100, and 10 cpg for the next 15 mmgy of B100 produced in a fiscal year. 60 months of eligibility per producer.	Biodiesel	Producer		Feedstock for plants must be 51% sourced from inside Missouri and 100% from inside the United States (MO Revised Statutes, 142.031).
Montana	Biodiesel production tax credit for increases in annual production of 10 cpg increase over the previous year (MT code 15-70-601).	Biodiesel			
Montana	PTC of 20 cpg for all production sourced from MT feedstocks. Eligibility requirements ramp up from 20% MT content in year one to 65% MT content in year 6. Credit is pro-rated downwards based on share of feedstocks originating from outside of the state. Incentive available during first six years of production; may not exceed $6m/year for state or $2m/yr per producer. (MT statutes 15-70-522).	Ethanol	PTC		Payments capped at $6m/yr per producer and $2m/yr per distributor (MT Code 15-70-522)
Nebraska	PTC of 18.5 cpg on first 15.625 MGY of ethanol production. Credit caps of up to $2.8m per year per plant, for eight years (a total of $22.5m/ plant). Plants must be producing by 30 June 2004 to be eligible (ACE, 28).	Ethanol	Producer	NE Department of Revenue estimates the cost of these tax credits at $100m to $176m for 2006 through 2012 when eligibility ceases (NE DOR, 2005). Changes to the rules, especially given large increases in production capacity, would result in much larger outlays. Credits granted from 1990 through 2005 were nearly 230m (NE DOR, 2006; url in source column).	
North Dakota	PTC of up to 40 cpg for ethanol produced and sold in ND. Plants built pre-07/01/95, get avg. of $450k/yr from 2005-07 if capacity <15 MGY. Plants >15 MGY get avg. of $225k/yr during same period (EERE, May 2006).	Ethanol			
North Dakota	Agricultural products utilization commission can also make quarterly counter-cyclical payments to ethanol producers depending on corn and ethanol prices under ND Code 4-14.1-08. (ACE, 35). These payments support increased production at plants built prior to 1 July 1995; or after 31 July 2003 (per ND 4-14.1-01).	Ethanol		Rate rises as corn prices rise or ethanol prices fall. Benchmarks not indexed for inflation.	Capacity increases must be the less of 10 mmgy or 50% of existing capacity. Total annual disbursements under this provision seem to be capped at $1.6m/year; with the most any facility can cumulatively earn at $10m (ND 4.14-1.09).

	Subsidy Description	Fuel	Cat	Subsidy Rate ($mils)	Comments/ Other Eligibility Criteria
Oklahoma	Biodiesel PTC of 20 cpg for new plant construction or capacity increases completed during the period of eligibility. Credits allowed for 5 years, ending before Dec. 31, 2011. Eligibility determined based on maintaining capacity utilization of 25% or more during first six months of operation. Caps of 25 mmgy for capacity prior to 2012; 10 mmgy thereafter. Lifetime limits per facility of credits on 125 mmg.	Biodiesel	Producer	Max of $25m/plant prior to 2012; $6m/ plant subsequent to 2012. PV would be lower.	Capacity expansions eligible prior to 2012 if equal to 12x the average of the 3 highest month production levels; or after 2012 if at least 2 mmgy. No size requirements for new construction. Credits must be approved by the tax authority.
Oklahoma	Ethanol PTC of 20 cpg for new plant construction or capacity increases completed during the period of eligibility. Credits allowed for 5 years, ending before Dec. 31, 2011. Eligibility determined based on maintaining capacity utilization of 25% or more during first six months of operation. (OK Statutes 68-2357.66).	Ethanol	Producer	Eligibility caps: single plant (25 mmgy pre-2011 plants; 10 mmgy post-2011 plants; max. 125 mmg lifetime eligibility. For industry, caps of 75 mmgy pre-2011; 30 mmgy post-2011.	Capacity expansions eligible only after Jan. 1, 2011, and only for substantial increases (roughly quadrupling).
Pennsylvania	Grants to ethanol producers of 5 cpg on up to 12.5 MGY can be provided by the PA DEP Alternative Incentive Grant Program (ACE, 39).				
South Dakota	PTC of 20 cpg through 12/31/06 capped at $1 mln per year per plant; total of $10 mln lifetime per plant. Maximum payout on PTCs under this provision (SD Statutes 10-47 B-162) of $7 million a year (ACE, 42).				
Tennessee	PTC of up to $6 million (ACE, 43). Couldn't find this referenced elsewhere.				
Texas	PTC of 20 cpg on first 18 MGY from each or biodiesel or ethanol plant. Corresponding fee levied on producers of 3.2 cpg on this same production level generates a net gain to them of 16.8 cpg. Fees go back to the TX Dept. of Agriculture to fund part of the PTC; the remainder of funding comes from the general fund. Plants eligible for 10 years of tax credits. (TX Ag Code 16.001 - 16.005).	Ethanol and Biodiesel	Producer	18 mmgy x 16.8 cpg net x 10 years = $30.2m per plant maximum.	All forms of biodiesel eligible. No restrictions on where the crop/ animal products need to be sourced from. No limits on how many plants a single owner can be subsidized for.
Virginia	Biofuels Production fund issues grants to biofuels producers, especially ethanol and biodiesel. Grants are 10 cpg that are sold in Virginia between 1 January 2007 and 1 January 2017. Minimum production size of 10 mmgy to be eligible, and can receive grants during 6 calendar years (VA Code 45.1.393 and 45.1-394). Pre-existing production eligible only if production in 2007 exceeds 2006 level by more than 10 mmgy, and stays at that level (or higher) in future years. This provision effectively allows all pre-existing production to receive the subsidy (EERE, May 2006).	Ethanol and Biodiesel	Producer		

	Subsidy Description	Fuel	Cat	Subsidy Rate ($mils)	Comments/ Other Eligibility Criteria
Wisconsin	PTC of 20 cpg on first 15 MGY of ethanol production; capped at $3 million over 5 years. Expired 1 July 2006. Eligibility period of 5 yrs; minimum production threshold of 10 MGY/year; and commodity inputs for the plant must come from within WI. Availability subject to legislative funding (ACE, 50).	Ethanol			
Wyoming	PTC of 40 cpg, up to a maximum of $4m/year for the entire state or $2m/yr for single plant. (Single plant max. is higher if certain expansion thresholds are met). Credits available through 30 June 2009. Plants built or expanded after 1 July 2003 get 15 years of credits. (ACE, 51; EERE, May 2006). WY 39-17-109.	Ethanol	Producer		At least 25% of the distillation feedstock purchases (excluding water) must originate from within WY to be eligible for the credit. Existing production prior to 1 July 2003 receive PTC only through 30 June 2009. Tax credits can be sold to anybody.

Grants, subsidized credit and tax concessions related to capital investment

	Subsidy Description	Fuel	Cat	Subsidy Rate ($mils)	Comments/ Other Eligibility Criteria
Federal	EPACT Sect. 251, Insular areas energy security. Funds decentralized energy sources. Includes coconut-based biofuels amongst eligible sources (EPACT 251).	Biodiesel, though lots of other fuels.		$6m/year authorized, for all fuels.	
Federal	Sec. 1510, Renewable Fuel Research and Production Grants, primarily to states generating potentially usable biomass but that don't have a large ethanol production base (EPACT 1510).	Ethanol		Authorized: $25m/ yr for 2006-2010 ($125m total)	
Federal	Sec. 1511, cellulosic biomass ethanol conversion assistance. Eligible facilities are non-profit sites such as universities (EPACT 1511).	Ethanol		Authorized: $250m in 2006; $400m in 2007.	According to EESI (July 06), the Senate clarified language for loan guarantees on Sec. 1511(b) to allow private financing of the risk premium normally covered by DOE, with the federal government insuring the entire project. If this makes DOE less of a gate-keeper in screening out projects, it could be a substantial taxpayer risk.
Federal	Sec. 1512, Grants to producers to help build cellulosic ethanol plants (EPACT 1512).	Ethanol	Producer	Authorized: $100m in 2006; $250m in 2007; $400m in 2008.	
Federal	USDA Sect. 9006 Renewable Energy Systems and Energy Efficiency Improvements Funding			Separate sheet.	
Delaware	Green Energy Fund, administered by the State Energy Office, to provide loans and grants for a variety of clean energy projects. Includes biodiesel manufacturing facilities.	Biodiesel	Producer		Grants capped at 25% of project cost; no single project can receive more than $300,000 (EERE, May 2006).
Illinois	Renewable fuel plant development funding of $20m passed the IL legislature in May 2006. To be run via DCEO, the money is slated to expedite the construction of biorefineries for ethanol and biodiesel.	Both	Grant	$20m	

	Subsidy Description	Fuel	Cat	Subsidy Rate ($mils)	Comments/ Other Eligibility Criteria
Iowa	General investment tax credit provides an ITC equal to the percentage of the new investment "directly related to new jobs created by the location or expansion of an eligible business under the program." This includes a wide range of plant, real estate, and machinery purchases. Most businesses must amortize the credit in five equal installments, with carryforwards of up to 7 years. Value-added agricultural processors and ethanol producers (specifically named) are allowed to request a refund for unused tax credits (IA Code, Title 1, Subtitle 5, 15.333).	Ethanol, appears biodiesel as well.	Producer		ITC refunds require issuance of a tax credit certificate from the state. The state caps issuance of such certificates at $4m per year. Unclear how this provision interacts with the other production subsidies in the state. Rules on the program changed in 2005. New rules not that different in terms of rates or caps (See IA Admin. Code, 701-52.28(15)).
Iowa	Value-Added Agricultural Products and Processes Financial Assistance Program, started in 1994, has provided nearly $45 million in public subsidies to a variety of projects that "encourage the increased utilization of agricultural commodities produced in the State of Iowa." This has included renewable energy since its inception. Ethanol facilities have been regular recipients of this support (IA DED, 2005; IA Code Title 1, Subtitle 5, 15E.111).	Ethanol, Biodiesel, other biomass fuels		Don't know total funding to these sectors from the overall grants of $45m.	
Kentucky	KY Agriculture Development Fund offers grants to new projects, including ethanol production plants (Kotrba, Feb. 2006)	Ethanol	Producer		
Louisiana	Property and equipment used to manufacture, produce or extract B100 is exempt from from state sales and use taxes (EERE, May 2006).	Biodiesel	Producer		
Minnesota	Economic recovery grants via the MN Department of Trade and Economic Development were also given to ethanol plants.	Ethanol	Producer	Through FY96, grants of $150k each went to Morris Ag Energy, Corn Plus (Winnebago) and Heartland Corn Products (Winthrop). A grant of $100k went to Al-Corn (Claremont). (MN OLA, p. 7).	
Montana	Tax credit of 15%, up to $500,000, for investments into oil seed crushing facilities. (MT code 15-32-701).	Biodiesel		No operating ethanol or biodiesel plants currently in state.	Facility must be operating prior to 1 January 2010.
Montana	All manufacturing machinery, fixtures, equipment, and tools used for the production of ethanol from grain during the course of the construction of an ethanol manufacturing facility and for 10 years after initial production of ethanol from the facility are exempt from property taxes (MT Code 15-6-20).	Ethanol	Production		
New Mexico	Compensating tax exemption for equipment related to ethanol or biofuels production. The compensating tax acts as a use or excise tax on real property, and is 5% in NM (DSIRE database; NM HB 995).	Ethanol, biodiesel	Production	5% x cost of equipment.	

	Subsidy Description	Fuel	Cat	Subsidy Rate ($mils)	Comments/ Other Eligibility Criteria
New York	Grants for biodiesel refining facilities. Total funding of $500k through the NY State Energy Research and Development Authority, with maximum grants of $100k/recipient. A wide variety of planning, development and operational costs are eligible. (Pataki, 20 November 2005).	Biodiesel	Grant	$500k	
New York	Grant subsidy for 50 mmgy dry mill ethanol plant in New York state. Total cost of $87m.	Ethanol	Grant	$3.1m for rail access; $2.5m in economic development funding. $25m in additional federal support through USDA; and $0.4m through the NY DOT have been requested (Pataki, 8 May 2006).	
New York	Funding grant for development of Cellulosic Ethanol Facility in New York. Program to be administered by the state Department of Agriculture and Markets (Pataki, 8 May 2006).	Ethanol	Grant	$20m	
North Carolina	A tax credit equal of 35% is available to taxpayers who construct, purchase, or lease renewable energy property. This includes equipment that uses renewable biomass to produce ethanol or biodiesel, as well as equipment for converting, conditioning, and storing the resultant fuels. Credit taken in 5 installments, being year property begins active service. Non-residential investments may earn no more than $2.5m in tax credits per installation.(NC statutes 105-129.15 and 105-129.16A) (EERE, May 2006).	Both	Production, infrastructure		Can offset a maximum of 50% of state tax liability under either the state franchise tax or the state income taxes. Firm must stipulate which tax to offset in first year of tax claimed; selection is binding. Tax credit carryforward of up to five years.
North Carolina	State grants to ethanol plant owned by the NC Grain Growers Cooperative from Golden LEAF, the state fund to reinvest proceeds from tobacco settlements. Additional grants to a biodiesel plant were also announced in 2002, but not funded thus far. Grants to the ethanol plant are mired in conflicts of interest amongst the principals, and an attempt to transfer the assets to a related private owner. (Carrington, 2003).	Ethanol, biodiesel		$1.1m in grants to the coop through 2003. $10m commitment to biodiesel plant hadn't been funded as of 2003.	
North Dakota	Biodiesel equipment used to facilitate sale of biodiesel (B2 or higher) in the state is exempt from state sales tax (EERE, May 2006; ND Code 57-39.2-04(51))	B2 or higher.		Normal sales tax is 5%.	
North Dakota	Biodiesel equipment tax credit of 10% per year for five years (total credit of 50%) of the cost of enabling a facility to sell B2 or higher.	Biodiesel		Capped at 50k per facility.	
North Dakota	Income tax credits of 25% (up to a maximum of 250k) for investing in a qualified ND venture capital corporation (ND Code 10-30.1). Venture capital is now a significant source of funding for ethanol and biodiesel plants.	Ethanol, biodiesel			

	Subsidy Description	Fuel	Cat	Subsidy Rate ($mils)	Comments/ Other Eligibility Criteria
North Dakota	Subsidies to agricultural commodity processing facilities. These are any plants that apply knowledge and/or labor to boost the value of agricultural products produced in ND. Would include ethanol and biodiesel. Investment tax credit of 30% of investment, up to $50k per year per taxpayer, $250k total for a project. (ND Code 57-38.6). Sales tax exemption for coal if used in an ag processing facility or sugar beet refining facility (ND Code 57-39.2-02.1(g). Construction materials used to construct an agricultural processing facility are exempt from sales and use taxes (of 5%) (ND Code 57-39.2-04.4).	Ethanol, probably biodiesel as well.			Pass-through entities defined at the taxpayer for the purposes of the ITC limits.
Oklahoma	Agricultural producer tax credit of 30% for investments, by farmers, in value-added agricultural processing. Generally capped at $2m/year per facility (OK Statutes 68-2357.25).	Appears to include ethanol and biodiesel.	Producer		
Oregon	Property tax exemption for ethanol facilities equal to 50% of the assessed value. Subsidy lasts 5 years (ORS 307.701; OR DEP 2006).	Ethanol	Producer		
Oregon	Business energy tax credits equal to 35% of the eligible project costs. Includes a range of alternative energy investments, including ethanol and biodiesel. Max. credit per project of $10m. Includes most investment costs (including loan fees), other than maintenance costs (Sources in last column).	Ethanol, Biodiesel	Producer		
Pennsylvania	Grant for biodiesel injection blending facility in Middletown, PA, via the PA Energy Harvest Grant Program (Rendell, October 2005).	Biodiesel	Grant	220k	
South Dakota	Biodiesel production facility tax refund for excise, sales, or use taxes paid by contractors for products used to build a new agricultural processing facility. While the project must include an expansion to an existing soybean processing facility that will be used to produce biodiesel to get the refund, it appears that taxes on the entire project (not just the biodiesel part) will be refunded. Project costs must be $4.5m or greater (EERE, May 2006).	Biodiesel	Producer		
Utah	Corporate tax credit of 10% of eligible investments, up to a maximum of 50k. Includes biomass, but only if converted into electrical energy.				
Washington	Tax exemption for alternative fuels distribution and sale infrastructure. All equipment, services, and vehicles associated with the sale or distribution of ethanol (E85 and above) and biodiesel (B20 and above) are exempt from state retail fuel sales and use taxes. (EERE, May 2006; Washington Revised Code 82.08.955). State taxes in effect for 2006 are 6.5% on most items; and 6.8% on retail motor vehicles.	B20, E85	Infrastructure	6.5 to 6.8% of the cost of investments in biofuels infrastructure and delivery.	

	Subsidy Description	Fuel	Cat	Subsidy Rate ($mils)	Comments/ Other Eligibility Criteria
Washington	Tax deferral of state and local sales and use taxes through 1 July 2009 for investments in biofuels production capacity. Includes buildings, equipment, labor to make biodiesel, biodiesel feedstock, and alcohol fuel. Qualifying buildings and equipment are also exempt from state and local property and leasehold taxes for six years. A reduced Business and Occupation tax rate of 0.138% applies to the people involved with these activities.			Standard business and occupation rate is 0.484 (WA statute 82.04.240). Standard sales and use tax rate is 6.5%.	
Arkansas	Income tax credit for biodiesel supply chain, up to 5% of the cost of facilities and equipment.	Biodiesel	Infrastructure		
Arkansas	State income tax credit for investment in production of advanced biofuels (as of 2001). State rebate for incremental cost of alternative fuel vehicles, also as of 2001 (CEC, 23).	Ethanol, Biodiesel			
Indiana	Government support for Indiana Bio-Energy LLC plant in Bluffton, IN. $800,000 in annual support guarantees in case of project default, funded by local governments through County Economic Development Income Tax Funds. State cash and training grants of ~$1.6m. Planned state funding for infrastructure improvements near the site (Frank, 2006).	Ethanol	Producer		
Iowa	Iowa Renewable Fuel Fund provides low cost financing for renewable energy projects, often ethanol or biodiesel. 20% of commitment is a soft-loan (i.e., grant); 80% is a low-interest (below prime rate) loan. Maximum loan per recipient is 520k (EERE, May 2006; Iowa Energy Center). Run through the Value-Added Agricultural Products and Processes Financial Assistance Program.	Ethanol (and others)		$44m in funding between 1995–2005. Ethanol share of total awards not known (IA DED, 2005).	
Iowa	Alternate Energy Revolving Loan Program is accessible to any individual or organization who wants to build renewable energy production facilities in Iowa. Recipients get a combination of AERLP funds and private lender funds (IA Energy Center, 2006).			Public funding may comprise up to 50% of the loan, but no more than 250k per project. Interest rates can be as low as 0%. No information on whether the privately-funded portion of the loan is also state guaranteed.	
Kentucky	$300,000 loan to Commonwealth Agri-Energy, LLC for construction of ethanol plant in Hopkinsville, KY. Funded by the Christian County Fiscal Court, not by the state (Alt. Fuels Today, 2 February 2004).	Ethanol	Producer		

	Subsidy Description	Fuel	Cat	Subsidy Rate ($mils)	Comments/ Other Eligibility Criteria
Minnesota	Ethanol Production Facility Loan Program, begun in 1993, provided up to 500k/facility to help finance construction and start-up. Loans had supported seven facilities in the state through 2002 (Rankin, 2002). MN issues municipal revenue bonds for this purpose (MN statutes 41B.044). Stock loan program. Seven facilities also made use of low interest state loans to farmers from the Rural Finance Authority to pay for up to 45% of the costs of shares of stock in a value-added agricultural product processing facility (Rankin, 2002). The interest rate subsidy on these was about 4% (MN OLA, p. 7).	Ethanol	Producer	As of 1997, the four dry mills in the state had each received a low-interest MN loan for $500k, as well as up to $1m in tax increment financing per plant (MN OLA, p. xi). Through the end of FY97, at total of $466k in loans had been made, "most of these to purchase stock in ethanol plants." (MN OLA, p. 7).	
Missouri	Authorized up to $250m in non-taxable revenue bonds to assist Renewable Power build a 40 mmgy ethanol plant in Cape Girardeau County (Alt. Transport Fuels Today, 4 December 2003). Not clear why so much capacity has been released since the projected cost of the plant was only $58 million.	Ethanol	Producer	Large intermediation value.	
Nebraska	Skip zoning, allowed smaller cities to collect property taxes from nearby plants, then use these dollars to help with project financing. (Werner, 20).				Not clear if applied to biodiesel and ethanol plants, or just biomass-fired electricity.
North Dakota	Biodiesel loan program via the Partnership in Assisting Community Expansion buys down interest rate on loans for biodiesel production facilities. Eligible purposes include purchase of real property and equipment, expansion of facilities, working capital, and inventory. Size of program noted at $1.2 million.	Biodiesel			
Oregon	Energy Loan Program (SELP) provides low-interest loans for a variety of alternative energy programs including biofuels (OR DEP, 2006).	Ethanol, Biodiesel			
Federal	Sect. 1510 Cellulosic biomass loan guarantee program. Loan guarantees for up to 20 years to finance plants that convert municipal solid waste or cellulosic biomass into ethanol. May support up to three plants (EPACT 1510).	Ethanol	Producer	Authorizes "such sums as may be necessary." Up to 80% of cost, not exceeding $250m/ project.	Performance bond of at least 20% of amount borrowed is required. Guarantee fee also charged to cover administrative costs. Max. value, excluding defaults = $250m per project x 80% max guarantee x 4 projects max x 2.5% avg. int. rate spread btwn Corp Baa and treasury debt (2000–2005), or $20m/year. CBO estimated cost of this program assuming 3 loans at $110m over 5 yrs, or $22m/yr.

	Subsidy Description	Fuel	Cat	Subsidy Rate ($mils)	Comments/ Other Eligibility Criteria
Federal	EPACT 1516, Sugar-based ethanol loan guarantee program. Offers guarantee on up to 80% of the project cost (max. of $50m per project). Supplemental guarantees for cost increases boost total coverage to as high as 95% of the original cost estimate (EPACT 1516). Estimates here assume four projects nationwide.			$4m	Guarantee enables risky borrowers to obtain debt at the Treasury rate. New industry debt rate would be Baa or worse. We assume Baa, 80% of $50m project. Guarantee cuts borrowing costs by ~2.5%. Subsidy shown is per per year for 4 projects. Rises linearly if more are done.
Federal	EPACT Title XVII. Loan guarantees for advanced energy projects, including biomass. Most of energy must be converted to electricity. However, 1703(a)(2) allows industrial gasification projects in which 65% of biomass is converted into electricity, and up to 35% can go to gas products used as a fuel of feedstock. This may open the provision to benefit biodiesel or ethanol production (EPACT, 1701-1703). Biofuels are eligible per p. 2 of DOE solicitation.	Biodiesel and ethanol (and others)	Producer	Fees under wide discretion of the secretary of DOE.	Max. term of 30 years or 90% of the useful project life, whichever is less. Guarantee capped at 80% of the project cost. Total guarantees under this traunche capped at $2 billion. For the purposes of estimating the subsidy value, we assume 15% will go to cellulosic ethanol.
California	Agricultural Industries Energy Program. Subsidized loan program for a variety of uses including ethanol production facilities (CA Public Resources Code 25650).			At least 2% below rate earned in CA Pooled Money Investment Account.	Max. duration of 7 years.
Hawaii	Authorized $50m in special-purpose revenue bonds to fund a baggasse-fed ethanol plant in Kauai, run by the World Wide Energy Group. Bonds were authorized in 2000, with a sales deadline recently extended to 2008 (Sommer, 2004).	Ethanol	Producer	Rev. loss estimate per year = face value x muni bond rate x marg. tax rate.	Revenue bonds not guaranteed by the state, but are tax exempt and greatly reduce the plant's cost of borrowing.
Nebraska	Authorizes public power districts to finance and/or build ethanol production and distribution capacity. Authorizes use of tax exempt municipal bonds for the construction of such plants (NE Statutes 70-143).	Ethanol	Production		
New Jersey	Tax-exempt bond financing for ethanol production plants via the New Jersey Economic Development Authority. $84 million financing approved in late 2005 for a 52 mmgy plant owned by Future Fuels, Inc. in Toms River, NJ. No information on other NJEDA loan or financing commitments (Nuclear Solutions, 2005).	Ethanol	Production	$84m in tax-exempt financing. Rev. loss estimate per year = face value x muni bond rate x marg. tax rate.	

	Subsidy Description	Fuel	Cat	Subsidy Rate ($mils)	Comments/ Other Eligibility Criteria
Montana	New or expanded industry tax credit. Businesses engaged in the production of energy by means of an alternative renewable energy source are eligible for the new or expanded industry tax credit against corporate income tax (MT Code 15-31-124 et. seq.)				To be considered an expanding industry, total full-time jobs must increase by 30 per cent or more. The credit is equal to 1 per cent of new wages paid in state during the first three years of operation. No carry back or carryover is allowed for this credit.
Oregon	Enterprise zone tax exemptions from property taxes for site improvements for 3 or 5 years. (OR Code 285C.055; OR DEP, 2006).				
Federal	USDA Sec. 6401 Value-Added producer grants			Separate sheet; fairly small.	
Iowa	Consultant support for bioenergy business plans through the Rural Economic Value-Added Mentoring Program. Low cap to subsidy suggests this program will primarily support very small on-farm conversion programs rather than large plants (IA DNR, 2006).	Ethanol, biodiesel		Max. of $10k grant per approved project in consulting support.	
Subsidies to intermediate inputs (goods or services)					
Arkansas	Rice Straw Income Tax Credit (Ark Code Ann 26-51- 512). Tax credit of $15/ton of rice straw, in excess of 500 tons, purchased by an Arkansas end user for use in processing, manufacturing, generating energy, or producing ethanol. (AR DFA, 2005). Estimated cost for 2006–07 is 2.5m (AR DFAb, 2005).	Ethanol	Producer	~1.2m/year. Will rise steeply if rice-to-ethanol plant now being researched is built.	Credit limited to 50% of the income tax due for the tax year. Unused credits can be carried forward for 10 years (AR DFA, 2005).
Government-funded research, development, demonstration and market promotion					
Federal	Sec. 971(d), Integrated bioenergy research centers. Funding via DOE's Office of Science.	Various biofuels		$49m/yr authorized for 2005 2009.	Split 50% cellulosic, 25% starch, 25% biodiesel (guess).
Illinois	Ethanol research on corn-to-ethanol conversion efficiency at Western Illinois University.	Ethanol	Grant	$1 million	
New York	Funding through the NY Dept. of Agriculture and Markets Food and Agricultural Industry Development Grants for biodiesel projects at Sidor Farms and Northern Biodiesel of 60k each in 2006 (Pataki, 8 May 2006).	Biodiesel	Grant	120k	
New York	Funding through the NY Dept. of Agriculture and Markets Food and Agricultural Industry Development Grants for cellulosic ethanol crop research at SUNYESF and Cornell (Pataki, 8 May 2006).	Ethanol	Grant	82k	
Federal	EPACT Sec. 208 Sugar cane ethanol program, to be run out of EPA. Demonstration projects on sugar-based ethanol production, with funds split equally between the states of HI, LA, FL, and TX (EPACT section 208).	Ethanol	Producer	Authorized: $36m over 3 years.	
Federal	EPACT Sect. 757, Biodiesel Engine Testing program. Public/private partnership to test engine and fuel injection systems to better handle bio-diesel blends (EPACT 757).	Biodiesel		Authorized: $5m/yr, 2006–2010; $25m total.	
Federal	EPACT 941, amendments to the Biomass Research and Development Act of 2000 modify language to include biofuels in many of the provisions of the original law (EPACT 941).	Both		Unknown.	

	Subsidy Description	Fuel	Cat	Subsidy Rate ($mils)	Comments/ Other Eligibility Criteria
Federal	EPACT Section 946 Pre-Processing and Harvesting Demonstration Grants. Funds research into harvesting and processing of biomass that is subsequently used to make ethanol or other energy (EPACT 05, Sect. 946).	Ethanol, probably biodiesel as well.	Producer	Authorized $5m per year, 2006–2010.	Split between ethanol and biodiesel.
Federal	EPACT Sect. 1505. Mandated study of health effects of fuel additives, many of which are related to ethanol (EPACT 1505).	Ethanol	Producer	No data	
Federal	Sect. 1511 cellulosic biomass research facilities at Mississippi State University and Oklahoma State University (EPACT 1511).	Ethanol		$4m/yr., 2005–07.	
Federal	EPACT 1514, Advanced biofuels technologies program. Funding demonstration projects with at least 4 different cellulosic to ethanol Conversion technologies; and not less than 5 approaches to develop marketable byproducts. (EPACT 1514).	Ethanol		Authorized: $110m for 2005–09 ($550m total)	
Federal	EPACT 932(d) integrated biorefinery demonstration projects. Though fuels are a key output of the biorefineries, the model is a petrochemical refinery that produces a range of outputs to supply multiple industries. Up to 3 demonstration projects to be funded, with a 60% cost-share funded by the industrial partner (Stevens, 2/22/2006; EERE, 2005, "Integrated biorefineries")			160m over 3 years as announced. Funding in statute restricted to no more than $100m per demonstration facility. Funding announcement Summer 2006 estimated $57m in funding for 2007.	Requires use of ligno-cellulosic feedstocks. Not only for energy; integrated production of other chemicals as well. We assume 50% of funding will support energy production; 50% for other productions.
Federal	EPACT 932(f), University Biodiesel Program. Studies the performance of biodiesel blends up to B100, containing high cellulosic content. (EPACT 932(f)). Focus on use of biodiesel in university-owned electric power generating stations.	Biodiesel		No amounts specified.	
Federal	2002 Farm Bill, Section 9008. USDA/DOE biomass research and development grants support a variety of rural energy options including biofuels (EESI, 2004).	Ethanol, biodiesel	Producer	~$3m awarded for ethanol research in 2004.	Biodiesel eligible, but no awards visible in the year for which we reviewed data.
Federal	R&D via standard DOE budget; and via the Biomass R&D Act of 2000.				
Illinois	Illinois Renewable Fuels Research, Development, and Demonstration Program, run through the IL Department of Commerce and Economic Opportunity (EERE, May 2006). Promotes and expands the use of ethanol in transportation.	Ethanol	Grant	Funding in 2003 of $750k; in 2004 of $400k.	Grant maximums are 25k for planning/ development; 350k for demonstration and research/development projects. Demonstration projects by for-profit entities require 50% cost share; all others have no required cost-share (IL OAG, 2006).
Illinois	Corn-to-ethanol research pilot plant, managed by the IL Ethanol Research Advisory Board. Funded jointly by the Federal and State of IL governments.	Ethanol	Grant	Initial funding, 2004: $15m fed, $6m state. 2004 additional: 0.6m state 2005: 1.0m state, 2m fed 2006: 4m state. Total known: $28.6m	

	Subsidy Description	Fuel	Cat	Subsidy Rate ($mils)	Comments/ Other Eligibility Criteria
New York	$20m grant available to finance construction of pilot cellulosic ethanol plants. Funds can go to 1–4 projects, depending on responses (EESI, July 2006, p. 16).	Ethanol	Grant	$20m	
Federal	Sect. 1506, Analysis of Motor Vehicle Fuel Changes to study emissions profile of new fuel blends, primarily with ethanol.	Ethanol		No data	
Oklahoma	Biodiesel Development Advisory Committee, 11 member group from various backgrounds to study and promote increased use and production of biodiesel within Oklahoma. (OK Statutes, Title 2, 37B-1950.11)	Biodiesel	Producer		
Oklahoma	Ethanol Development Advisory Committee, 15 member group from various backgrounds to study and promote increased use and production of ethanol within Oklahoma. (OK Statutes, Title 2, 37A-1950.2)	Ethanol	Producer		
Federal	EPACT945 Regional Bioeconomy Development Grants to support bioeconomy development associations, farm or energy trade associations or Land Grant institutions in study and support bioeconomy development.			$1m year.	
Federal	EPACT 947 Education and Outreach to producers and consumers, regarding both biofuels and bioproducts.	Both		Authorized $1m/year.	
Delaware	Funding from DE Soybean Board for rebates and marketing, promotion and education assistance (EERE, May 2006).	Biodiesel	Producer		
Minnesota	Minnesota E85 Team – public/private partnership to pilot large scale promotion of E85 (EERE, May 2006).	E85	Consumer		
Minnesota	Ethanol education to public, via MN Department of Agriculture. Funded from 1987 through 1998.	Ethanol		$100k/year, or roughly $1.1m over the life of the program. (Rankin, 2002).	
Nebraska	National Ethanol Board appointed and funded by the state to promote ethanol. State also authorized to fund memberships in national ethanol promotion organizations (NE Statutes, 66-1335).	Ethanol			
Washington	Biofuels Education fund establish a biofuels consumer education and outreach program at Washington State University extension energy program.	Biodiesel		0.1m	Funding data for one year; subsequent funding unknown.
Consumption subsidies					
Iowa	Biodiesel purchase grants funded by the sale of Energy Policy Act credits, will be used to fund the purchase of biodiesel for the IA Dept. of Transportation vehicles (EERE, May 2006)	Biodiesel	Consumer		
Louisiana	B100 used as fuel by a registered manufacturer in the state is exempt from state sales and use tax (EERE, May 2006).	Biodiesel	Producer		
Maryland	Biodiesel rebate to consumers for up to 50% of the incremental cost to purchase the biodiesel blend. Minimum rebate of $100; maximum of $1,000. Each consumer is eligible for only one year of rebate (EERE, May 2006).	Biodiesel	Consumer	Funded by farmers, not government, so program does not constitute a public subsidy (See www.mdsoy.org).	

	Subsidy Description	Fuel	Cat	Subsidy Rate ($mils)	Comments/ Other Eligibility Criteria
Missouri	Biodiesel purchase subsidies for school districts purchasing B20 or higher from non-profit generation cooperatives. Subsidies given to schools, but effectively supporting producers.	Biodiesel	Producer		
Montana	Retailer tax rebate of 1 cpg of biodiesel (50 cpg B100) purchased from a licensed distributor and if sourced entirely within MT (EERE, May 2006; MT Code 15 70-369).	Biodiesel	1 cpg		
New Jersey	Biodiesel fuel use rebate compensates state and . local government entitites for the incremental cost of using biodiesel over regular diesel.	Biodiesel	Consumer		
New York	Residential bioheat income tax credit. Provides 1 cent state income tax credit for each percentage of biodiesel blended into heating oil, not to exceed 20 cpg (Pearson, 30 May 2006).	Biodiesel	Consumer		Took effect July 2006.
North Carolina	Purchase subsidies to state agencies to offset the incremental cost of alternative fuels for their fleets (EERE, May 2006). NC Statutes 143-58.4, 143-58.5, 136-28.13, 143-341(8)i.	B20 or higher; E85 or higher; plus others.	Consumer		
Wisconsin	Funding to cover incremental cost of biodiesel usage in school buses is available through the Wisconsin Department of Public Instruction. (EERE, May 2006).	Biodiesel	Consumer		Shortfalls in funding vs. need for biodiesel subsidy would be allocated across recipient districts by the number of pupils.

Subsidies for infra-structure related to biofuel distribution

	Subsidy Description	Fuel	Cat	Subsidy Rate ($mils)	Comments/ Other Eligibility Criteria
Federal	EPACT Section 1342, Credit for Installation of Alternative Refueling Stations. Covers 30% of eligible cost of depreciable property, up to a 30k maximum (EPACT 1342).	E85 or higher; B20 or higher	Infrastructure	Estimated on Fed Tax page.	
Colorado	State income tax credits for installing E85 fueling equipment (NECV), and for alternative fueled vehicles (as of 2001) (CEC, 23).				
Illinois	State income tax credits for installing E85 fueling equipment (NECV).	Ethanol			
Illinois	E85 refueling infrastructure grants disbursed through the IL Dept. of Commerce and Economic Opportunity (EERE, May 2006).	Ethanol	Grant	$500k	Up to 50% of the cost to convert an existing site (up to 2k/site) or for construction of a new refueling facility (up to 40k/site).
Indiana	Biofuels Grants Program promotes increased use of biofuels in Indiana. Supports grants to install E85 and B20 infrastructure, or for school districts or large fleet operators to boost usage (EERE, May 2006).	Both	Infrastructure		Requires 50% matching funds. Maximum grants of 25k for single fuel infrastructure; 50k is both E85 and B20 being installed.
Iowa	Biodiesel Terminal Infrastructure Installation Grant provides cost share via the IA Department of Economic Development to install on-site and off-site terminals for biodiesel (IA Code 15.401; IA DNR 2006). State has appropriated $13m over next three years (2006-08) for this program. See: http://www.iowarfa.org/NR060705.php	Biodiesel	Infrastructure	Max of $30k for retailer per project; $50k for blender per project (EERE, May 2006).	

	Subsidy Description	Fuel	Cat	Subsidy Rate ($mils)	Comments/ Other Eligibility Criteria
Iowa	E85 cost-sharing with state government, to a maximum outlay of 325k/yr (EERE, May 2006). Has recently been used to fund new E85 pumps. (EPM, May 2006).	Ethanol	Infrastructure	325k/yr., though legislature "appears poised to increase the funding amount by between $2 million and $5 million" for FY2007 (EPM, May 2006).	
Kansas	State income tax credits for installing E85 fueling equipment (NECV). These equal 50% of total cost (max. of $200k per station) for in-service dates of 1 January 1996-1 January 2005. Credit caps after Jan. 1, 2005 are 40% of total cost (max. of $160k/station) (KS statutes 79-32, 201).	Ethanol (E70 or higher); probably biodiesel as well.	Infrastructure		
Kentucky	Grants for E85 stations (Kotrba, Feb. 2006).	Ethanol			
Maine	Tax credit for installation or upgrading of clean fuel or recharging stations for the public. Credit is equal to 25% of qualifying expenditures, through 31 December 2008 (EERE, May 2006).	Both	Infrastructure		
Minnesota	If the biodiesel mandate is repealed within eight years of enactment, distributors are eligible for partial reimbursement from the state for capital investments they made in blending infrastructure. Reimbursement rate is 80% in first two years, declining by 10% each successive year (MN Statutes, 239.771).	Biodiesel	Infrastructure		
Minnesota	Loans for installing ethanol pumps and infrastructure. No information on amounts, but considered an important element of the expansion in EERE's 2001 write-up (URL in source column).				
Montana	Tax credit to businesses and individuals for 15% of the cost of biodiesel storage and blending equipment. Credit limited to $52.5k for a distributor, and $7.5k for the owner of an outlet. (EERE, May 2006). MT 15-32-702.	Biodiesel			Credit must be taken in first year biodiesel is blended, and can't be carried forward.
Montana	Ethanol distributor credit.				
New Jersey	Local Government Alternative Fuel Infrastructure Program can reimburse the cost of installing alternative energy refueling infrastructure (including E85) up to 50k/applicant. 50% cost share required (EERE, MAy 2006).	E85	Infrastructure		
North Carolina	Tax credit for alternative fuel refueling infrastructure. 15% tax credit, taken in three equal installments. Includes pumps, tanks, other dispensing infrastructure. Does not seem to include trucks. 25% tax credit for renewable fuel processing facility, taken in seven equal installments (NC Statutes 105-129.16D).	E70 or above; Biodiesel of any blend ratio (per NC 105-449.60).	Infrastructure		
Ohio	Alternative Fuel Transportation Grant Program, funded by at least $1 million to increase biofuel infrastructure and availability within the state (EESI, July 2006, p. 9).	Both	Infrastructure	$1m minimum.	House Bill 245.
Ohio	Infrastructure grants to retail fuel station owners to install and promote E85 and/or B20 at their stations. Grants of up to $5k/recipient for E85; and $15k/recipient for B20. Funding through the Ohio Biofuels Retail Incentive Program (EERE, May 2006).	E85 and B20	Infrastructure	Maximum available funding of $135k through July 2006.	

	Subsidy Description	Fuel	Cat	Subsidy Rate ($mils)	Comments/ Other Eligibility Criteria
Oregon	State income tax credits for installing E85 fueling equipment (NECV).				
Tennessee	Grants through the TN Department of Transportation to install refueling network, including storage tanks and fuel pumps, dedicated to dispensing biofuels. Can fund capital costs of this equipment for private stations. Minimum private cost-share of 20%. (EERE, May 2006; TN DOT, 2006).	E85 or B20			
Subsidies to biofuel-consuming capital					
Federal	EPACT Sec. 741 Clean School Bus Program. Grants for up to 100% of retrofits and 50% of replacements for older, high-polluting school buses. E85- and biodiesel-fueled buses are eligible, among other propulsion systems (EPACT 05, Section 741).	E85, biodiesel	Infrastructure	Authorized: $55m in '06; $55m in '07; "such sums as necessary" for 2008–10.	Roughly 20% of past awards seem to have involved biodiesel. Virtually no ethanol.
Federal	EPACT Sec. 702. Diesel truck retrofit and fleet modernization program.	Biodiesel, other fuels as well		Authorized: $20m in 2006; $35m in 2007; $45m in 2008.	As with school bus program, we ascribe 20% of funding to biodiesel.
Federal	EPACT Sec. 791-97 Diesel Emissions Reduction. Cost share for improving emissions profile of existing diesel equipment.	Potentially biodiesel		$200m/yr for 2007–10.	Past funded projects focus on installation of pollution controls, not fuel substitution. Assume no benefit to biodiesel.
Colorado	Alternative fuel income tax credit for most of the incremental cost of purchasing an alternative-fueled vehicle. E85 eligibility specified; biodiesel eligibility via more general statute language. CO guidance suggests that in practice flex-fueled or dual-fueled vehicles have no incremental cost, so would not generate a tax credit (CO DOR, 2006).	Both	Infrastructure		
Georgia	Mandated purchase of alternative fueled vehicles for state agencies and departments; and for stocking ethanol and biodiesel at state refueling facilities. Mandates subject to economic tests and other language that suggest their effect in driving market behavior will be fairly weak (EERE, May 2006).	Both	Mandate		
Georgia	Tax credit for purchase of AFVs, including E85 or higher; or biodiesel. Credit equal to 10% of cost of new vehicle, conversion, or $2,500, whichever is less. Caps would be double for electric vehicles (EERE, May 2006; Georgia code 48-7-40.16).	E85 or higher; biodiesel			Definitions include "fuels other than alcohol derived from biological materials." This appears to include biodiesel, though not clear how mixtures of biological oils and standard diesel would be treated.
Hawaii	Allows each mandated purchase of an alternative fueled vehicle to be offset by use of equivalent to 450 gallons of B100 in existing state fleet (NBB, 25 May 2006).	Biodiesel	Purchase preference		

	Subsidy Description	Fuel	Cat	Subsidy Rate ($mils)	Comments/ Other Eligibility Criteria
Illinois	Purchase mandates, biodiesel. Any diesel powered vehicle, refueling at a bulk central refueling facility, that is owned or operated by any sub-national government entity (including schools and colleges) must use B2 when available. The only exceptions are if the vehicle can use a higher biodiesel blend or ultra low sulfur fuel. 625 IL Compiled Statutes 5/12-705.1). (EERE, May 2006).	Biodiesel	Mandate		
Kansas	State income tax credits for certain alternative fueled vehicles, including E85 and probably bio diesel. Credit ranges from 40% of cost/ incremental cost (max. $2.4k to $40k depending on vehicle weight) if placed in service after 1 January 2005. In-service from 1996-2004 was 50% (max 3k-50k, depending on vehicle weight) (EERE, May 2006; KS statutes 79-32, 201).	Ethanol (E70 or higher); probably biodiesel as well.	Infrastructure		
West Virginia	Alternative vehicle tax credits, including for E85 vehicles, of $3,750. Credit taken over three years, and was slated to expire in June 2006. (EERE, May 2006).	Ethanol			

Support for production of feedstocks

	Subsidy Description	Fuel	Cat	Subsidy Rate ($mils)	Comments/ Other Eligibility Criteria
Federal	2002 Farm Bill, section 2101. Allows Conservation Reserve Program land to be used to produce biomass for energy production, while still earning its CRP rental payment. (Schnepf, 18 May 2006, p. 13).	Ethanol and Biodiesel	Producer	Unknown	
Minnesota	Tax increment financing has been granted to most of the ethanol plants in the state as of 1996; (MN OLA, 7).				
Minnesota	Ethanol combustion efficiency grants provide $100k per year on ways to improve the efficiency of ethanol within vehicle systems. (MN Statutes 41A.09)	Ethanol	Producer	100k/yr.	Requires $2 of non-state money for each $3 of state money.
Federal	USDA sec. 9002 federal procurement of biobased products			Quite small.	
Arizona	State fleets must use or give preference to biodiesel blends when available (Pearson, 30 May 2006).	Biodiesel	Purchase preference		
Iowa	Biodiesel purchase mandates for state agencies at bulk fuel outlets. 5% renewable content by 2007, 10% by 2008, 20% by 2010 (EERE, May 2006).	Biodiesel	Mandate		
Iowa	Purchase mandates for state-funded refueling. Credit cards issued for refueling vehicles not allowed to be used for any fuel with less than E10 (IA Code Title VIII, Subtitle 1, 455A.6).	E10	Consumer		
Kansas	Biodiesel purchase preference for state-owned vehicles, so long as less than 10 cpg price premium.	Biodiesel (B2 or higher)	Mandate		
Minnesota	Executive order to expand availability and usage of E85 throughout the state; and to use E85 in state fleets whenever practical (Pawlenty, 2006).				

	Subsidy Description	Fuel	Cat	Subsidy Rate ($mils)	Comments/ Other Eligibility Criteria
Nebraska	Purchase mandates for state fleets of flex fuel or diesel vehicles, to buy E85 or biodiesel whenever "reasonably" available. Executive order 05-03 (EERE, May 2006).	E85, biodiesel	Consumer		
New Mexico	Purchase mandate for state agencies, universities and public schools. Must take action towards using ethanol and biodiesel to meet 15% of their total transportation fuel requirements (Executive order 2005-049, 2005) (EERE, May 2006)	Both	Mandate		
New York	Purchase mandates, through Executive Orders, mandate 5% of heating fuel used in state buildings be 2012 be biodiesel; and at least 2% of the fuels used in the state fleet be biodiesel, increasing to 10% by 2012 (Pataki, 20 November 2005).	Biodiesel	Mandate		
New York	Purchase mandate to use E85 in flex fuel state-fleets whenever feasible to do so. (EERE May 2006; Exec. order 142, 2005).	E85	Mandate		
North Carolina	State-owned fleets with >10 vehicles must achieve 20% reduction or displacement of current petroleum products consumed by 1 January 2010. Displacement by ethanol or biodiesel is eligible (EERE, May 2006).	Biodiesel, ethanol	Mandate		
Ohio	Purchase mandates for biofuels (1 million gpy of biodiesel and 30k gallons of ethanol) in state fleet; new Ohio light duty truck purchases must be able to drive on E85. Executive Order 2005-18T) (EERE, May 2006).	Both	Mandate		
Oregon	Purchase mandate for the city of Portland. City stations required to sell B5 and E10. (EESI, July 2006, p. 10).	Both	Mandate		
South Dakota	Purchase preference to stock and use B2 or higher for state employees and fleets. Executive order 2006-01 (EERE, May 2006).				
Virginia	Biodiesel purchase preference encourages state fleets to use biodiesel fuels. Fairly weak language though (EERE, May 2006).				
Wisconsin	Executive Order for state fleets to reduce the use of petroleum-based gasoline 20% by 2010, and 50% by 2015; and petroleum-based diesel 10% by 2010, and 25% by 2015. Also encourages increased education and usage of these fuels by state fleet operators (Doyle, 2006).	Ethanol and Biodiesel			
Colorado	Purchase mandate: by 10 July 2010, at least 10% of all state-owned bifuel vehicles to be fueled exclusively with alternative fuel. (EERE, May 2006).	Both	Mandate		
Iowa	Vehicle purchase mandates for state educational institutions. At least 10% of new car and light truck purchases must have alternative fueled propulsion (IA Code, Title VII, Sub. 2, 260C.19A).	E85 and higher; B20 and higher			

	Subsidy Description	Fuel	Cat	Subsidy Rate ($mils)	Comments/ Other Eligibility Criteria
Nevada	90% of the vehicles purchased by the state government or larger counties must be alternative fueled vehicles or ultra low emissions vehicles, starting in 2000. Targets can be met by converting existing fleet as well. Once purchased, the vehicle must operate solely on this alt fuel whenever it is available. Includes bus and heavy-duty vehicle fleets (EERE, 05/06, Nev. Statutes 486A.010 through 486A.180).	B5 or higher; probably E85 or higher (per NRS 590.020)	Infrastructure		Fleets containing less than 10 vehicles are exempt, but any fleet owned, leased, or operated by the government entity would be covered by this mandate. Other fuels also count; thus, entire incentive will not flow to biodiesel and ethanol.
New Jersey	Purchase mandate for NJ Transit Corp. All buses purchased after 1 July 2007 must run on alternatives to conventional diesel. Biodiesel buses (among other options) comply. (EERE, May 2006).	Biodiesel	Mandate		
North Carolina	State goal that 75% or more of new or replacement light duty cars and trucks purchased by the state after Jan. 1, 2004 must be AFVs or low emission vehicles. AFVs include E85 or "fuels, other than alcohol, derived from biological materials." (NC 143-215.107C).	E85, probably biodiesel	Purchase goal		
Ohio	State vehicles must all be flex-fuel cars. (EESI, July 2006, p. 9).	Both	Mandate		House Bill 245.
Federal	Rural Utility Services Plant financing (may be primarily electricity).			Unknown	
Montana	Oilseed crushing facility tax credit. Equals 15% of the cost of depreciable property used to crush oilseeds, up to a maximum of 500k (MT 15-32-701; Schumacher, 2006). Regulatory relaxation favoring biofuels.				
Illinois	Expedited permitting for ethanol and biodiesel plants.	Both	Grant	$100k	
Minnesota	Exemption from environmental impact assessment requirements for any plants with a production capacity of less than 125 mmgy, and located outside of the seven-county metropolitan area (MN Statutes, 116D.04, Subd. 2a).	Ethanol only	Production		
Minnesota	Construction of large energy facilities within the state of MN are not allowed to proceed without receiving a certificate of need from the state. Ethanol plants are exempt from this requirement (MN Statutes 216B.243).	Ethanol only	Producer		
Nebraska	Ethanol plants included among list of facilities that are included as "internal improvements." This inclusion makes them eligible to use state powers of eminent domain if they are not privately owned. May also have some additional rights even if privately owned. (NE Statutes, 70-667).	Ethanol	Production		
New Mexico	Added B20 or greater to state definition of "alternative fuel," making it eligible for other existing state programs. [need to figure out which] (EERE, May 2006).	B20			
Washington	Underground storage tanks holding B100 are exempt from regulations governing underground diesel tanks (EERE, May 2006).	Biodiesel			

	Subsidy Description	Fuel	Cat	Subsidy Rate ($mils)	Comments/ Other Eligibility Criteria
Renewable fuels mandate					
Federal	EPACT Section 1501, Renewable Content of Gasoline. Mandates minimum usage of ethanol in fuels at 4b gallons/yr in 2006, rising to 7.5 b gallons in 2012 (EPACT 1501).	Ethanol	Producer	Analyzed in Market Price Support	
California	Executive order setting targets for biofuels in the state. These targets are for 20% of the state's biofuels to be produced in-state by 2010, 40% by 2020, and 75% by 2050. Does not appear particularly binding, and percentages apply to shares of total biofuels usage, not to shares of total transportation fuel usage (CA Exec. Order, 2006).	Ethanol, biodiesel	Mandate	Probably small direct impact since terms do not appear to be particularly binding.	
Hawaii	10% ethanol content mandate for gasoline fuel. Some exemptions (HI Statutes, 486J-10).	Ethanol			
Iowa	Purchase mandate stipulating that 25% of a retailers fuel sales must be ethanol or biodiesel by 2020 (Pearson, 30 May 2006). Failure to reach target will reduce eligibility for tax credits.	Ethanol, biodiesel			Signed into law 30 May 2006. HF 2754 and HF 2759.
Maryland	Requires that, beginning FY08, at least 50% of the vehicles in the state fleet using diesel fuel use B5 or higher (NBB, 25 May 2006).	B5 or higher	Mandate		
Minnesota	State mandates that all diesel fuel sold in MN, used in internal combustion engines, must contain at least 2% biodiesel by value.	Biodiesel	Mandate	Incremental cost to consumers est. at $24m/yr for B2 mandate; $56m/yr for B5, and $56m/yr for B20. This was 2001$ and markets (Runge, 2002, v.) % increases from then (low) prices were: 4.5% for B2 mandate; 10.6% for B5; and 45% for B20 (Runge, 2002, 9). Runge notes that there would also be fairly large infrastructure investment costs.	
Minnesota	Ethanol mandated to comprise 10% of all gasoline sold in the state. This was increased to 20% in 2005, with a compliance date of 2013.	Ethanol	Mandate	In 1997, the state of MN estimated the ethanol mandate would cost consumers $33–50m/year, or 2–3 cpg (MN OLA, p. 14). However, they note that other estimates were as high as 5 cpg, and that adjusting for the lower energy content of ethanol blends generates an additional $24–$36 m/yr (1997$), p. xiv).	Higher mandate of 20% won't take effect if state reaches this level anyway by 2013. The rule would expire at the end of 2010 if Minnesota is not granted federal approval to use E-20 gasoline blends.
Missouri	Purchase preference for B20 or higher fuels in state vehicle fleet and heavy equipment, so long as B20 is within 25 cpg of straight diesel (EERE, May 2006).	Biodiesel			

	Subsidy Description	Fuel	Cat	Subsidy Rate ($mils)	Comments/ Other Eligibility Criteria
Missouri	Renewable Fuel purchase mandates for E10. Exclusions apply if more expensive than gasoline, and for premium gasoline blends. (EESI, July 2006, p. 10).	Ethanol	Mandate		
Montana	10% ethanol blending mandate once in-state production capacity hits 40 mmgy (ACE, 27; MT Code 82-15-121).	Ethanol	Mandate	No immediate impact, since in-state capacity below threshold.	Consumption of gasoline in MT (2001) was about 465mmgy, so the mandate could not be met by in-state supply.
Washington	2% purchase mandate for ethanol composition of gasoline beginning December 1, 2008. This could be increased to 10% if deemed not to affect air quality in the state. Mandate for 2% of diesel sold in Washington to be biodiesel beginning November 30, 2008, or when the state certifies in-state feedstock can support this mandate. Mandate rises to 5% once in-state production can meet 3% (EERE, May 2006).	Ethanol and Biodiesel	Mandate		
Iowa	Mandated all cars sold in the state needed to be able to operate on E10 or lower by 1993. (IA Code 331.908).	Ethanol			
Federal	USDA Sec. 2301 Environmental quality incentives program.			Unknown	

Sources:

Alt. Fuels Today, 3 December 2004. "Local MI [sic] Authority Approves Bonds for Ethanol Project," *Alternative Transportation Fuels Today*, 4 December 2003.

Alt. Fuels Today, 2 February 2004. "Local KY Court Approves Ethanol Plant Loan," *Alternative Transportation Fuels Today*, 2 February 2004.

AR DFA, 2005. Arkansas Department of Finance and Administration, Office of Excise Tax Administration, Tax Credits and Special Refunds Section. "Business Incentives and Credits," 2005. Downloaded from http://www.arkansas.gov/dfa/excise_tax_v2/et_tc_+B5'incentives.html, on 20 April 2006.

AR DFAb, 2005. Arkansas Department of Finance and Administration, "Major Actions that Affect Collections of Revenue in the 2005-07 Biennium," http://www.arkansas.gov/dfa/budget/documents/major_actions_affecting_collections.xls

Blagojevich, 2005. Blagojevich, Rod. Press Release, "Gov. Blagojevich Announces a Nearly $1 million Opportunity Returns Investment in Illinois' Emergy Biofuel Industry," Office of the Governor, 1 March 2005.

CA Exec. Order, 2006. California Executive Department, "Executive Order S-06-06 by the Governor of California," 29 April 2006.

Carrington, 2003. Carrington, Don. "Co-op Transfers Ethanol Plant to Private Group," *Carolina Journal*, 7 February 2003.

CO DOR 2006. Colorado Department of Revenue, Taxpayer Service Division, "FYI Income 9: Alternative Income Tax Credits," revised 3/13/2006. Downloaded from www.revenue.state.co.us/fyi/html/income09.html on 18 April 2006.

Doyle, 2006. Doyle, Jim. "Executive Order #141: Relating to Increased Utilization of Renewable Fuels in Vehicles Owned and Operated by the State of Wisconsin," 1 March 2006.

EERE, 2005. U.S. Department of Energy, Energy Efficiency and Renewable Energy Office. "Integrated Biorefineries," 12 October 2005 update.

EERE, 2006. U.S. Department of Energy, Energy Efficiency and Renewable Energy Office. Alternative Fuels Data Center, Incentives sort for all states, ethanol and biodiesel. Run 22 May 2006.

EESI, July 2006. Environmental and Energy Study Institute, "Bioenergy, Climate Protection, and Oil Reduction Newsletter," July 2006.

EPM, May 2006. "Iowa E85 fund looking at more money," *Ethanol Producers Magazine*, May 2006.

Frank, 2006. Frank, Geoff. "Wells Council Sends Strongly Worded Message to IBE on Ethanol Project Status," *The Bluffton (IN) News Banner*, 4 May 2006.

Heimdahl, 2006. Heimdahl, Matt. "Minnesota State Ethanol Subsidies," MN Taxpayers League, provided 6 June 2006.

HI Statutes. State of Hawaii, Statutes, sec. 235-110.3, accessed 22 May 2006.

IA Corn, 2006. Iowa Corn web site, "Ethanol Facts" accessed 6 October 2006. www.iowacorn.org/ethanol/ethanol_3a.html

IA DED, 2005. Iowa Department of Economic Development. "Value-Added Agricultural Products and Processes Financial Assistance Program," semi-annual progress report, FY2005.

IA DNR, 2006. Iowa Department of Natural Resources, "Financial Assistance and Incentives: Ethanol," www.iowadnr.com/energy/renewable/incentives/ethanol.html, accessed 30 May 2006.

IA Energy Center, 2006. Iowa Energy Center, "Financial Incentives for Developing Renewable Energy Facilities in Iowa," www.energy.iastate.edu/renewable/incentives/ accessed 30 May 2006.

ID Statutes. Idaho Statutes, 63-2402, "Imposition of Tax Upon Motor Fuel," and 63-2407,"Deductions Authorized." Downloaded from www.3state.id.us on 22 May 2006.

IL DCEO, RFDP, 2006. Illinois Department of Commerce and Economic Opportunity, "Renewable Fuels Development Program," accessed 30 May 2006.

IL Farm Bureau, 2006. Illinois Farm Bureau, "News Room: Senate OKs State Budget," 5 May 2006.

IL OAG. Illinois Office of the Auditor General, *Management and Program Audit, IL Department of Commerce and Economic Opportunity*, February 2006, pp. 85–99.

Iowa Energy Center. www.energy.iastate.edu/renewable/incentives/

Lambert, 2006. Lambert, Mark. Press Release, "State Budget Addresses Ethanol Expansion," Illinois Corn Growers Association, 4 May 2006.

MacDonald, 13 June 2006. Tom MacDonald, Fuels and Transportation Division, CA Energy Commission, e-mail to Doug Koplow, 13 June 06.

MN OLA, 1997. Minnesota Office of the Legislative Auditor, *Ethanol Programs: A Program Evaluation Report*, February 1997.

NBB, 25 May 2006. National Biodiesel Board, "2006 State Legislation Highlights Through May 25, 2006."

ND OSTC, 2005. North Dakota, Office of State Tax Commissioner, "Tax Incentives for Business," August 2005.

NE DOR, 2004. Nebraska Department of Revenue, Motor Fuels Division. "Changes to the Nebraska Monthly Fuel Tax Return, Form 73," 30 November 2004.

NE DOR, 2005. Nebraska Department of Revenue, Motor Fuels Division and The Nebraska Ethanol Board, "EPIC Report," December 2005.

Nuclear Solutions, 2005. Nuclear Solutions Press Release. "Approval for $84 Million in Bond Financing Officially Adopted by the State of New Jersey for Future Fuels, Inc. Ethanol Facility," 5 December 2005.

OK Statutes. Oklahoma Statutes Citationized, "Tax Credit for Eligible Biodiesel Facility," Title 68 section 2357.67, passed 1 July 2005.

OR DEP, 2006. Oregon Department of Energy, "Oregon State Incentives for Biofuels Production," from www.biofuels.4oregon.com/producers/stateincent, accessed 30 May 2006.

Pataki, 8 May 2006. Pataki, George. Press Release. "Government Announces Nearly $6m for New Ethanol Plant Development in WNY," 8 May 2006.

Pataki, 20 November 2005. Pataki, George. Press Release, "Governor Announces Initiatives to Increase Production and Use of Biofuels in New York State," 20 November 2005.

Pataki, 8 May 2006. Pataki, George. Press Release. "Governor: Cellulosic Ethanol has Great Potential in New York State," 8 May 2006.

Pawlenty, 2006. Pawlenty, Tim. "Governor Pawlenty Signs Executive Order Increasing Use of Renewable Fuels by State Agencies," 10 March 2006. Executive Order 06-03.

Pearson, 30 May 2006. Pearson, Amber. "Iowas Passes Broad Biodiesel Legislation; Other States Also Pass Bills to Increase Use of the Cleaner Burning Fuel," National Biodiesel Board press release, 30 May 2006.

Rankin, 2002. Rankin, Sam. "The Ethanol Industry in Minnesota," October 2002. Minnesota House of Representatives web site, www.house.leg.state.mn.us/hrd/issinfo/ssethnl.htm. Accessed 30 May 2006.

Rendell, November 2005. Rendell, Edward. Press Release. "Governor Rendell Leading Efforts to Lessen Nation's Dependence on Foreign Oil," October 2005.

Runge, 2002. Runge, C. Ford. *Minnesota's Biodiesel Mandate: Taking from Many, Giving to Few*, 15 February 2002. Prepared for the MN Trucking Association and the Biodiesel by Choice Coalition.

Schnepf, 15 May 2006. Schnepf, Randy. *Agriculture-Based Renewable Energy Production*, Congressional Research Service, 18 May 2006. RL32712.

Schuling, December 2005. Schuling, Mark. IA Department of Revenue, *Report on Progress in Developing a System to Track and Analyze Tax Credits*, Dec. 30, 2005. http://www.state.ia.us/tax/taxlaw/IDRTaxCreditReportDec2005.pdf

Sommer, 2004. Sommer, Anthony. "Ethanol bill heads to committee," *Honolulu Star-Bulletin*, 25 April 2004.

Stevens, 22 February 2006. Stevens, Craig. "DOE Announces $160 Million for Biorefinery Construction and Highlights New Agricultural Program to Promote Biofuels," U.S. Department of Energy Office of Public Affairs, 22 February 2006.

TN DOT 2006. Tennessee Department of Transportation, "Biofuels Refueling Infrastructure Funding Project: Application Package," 2006.

Werner 2006. Werner, Carol. "North Carolina Bioenergy Summit: Minnesota Model," Environmental & Energy Study Institute, 12 April 2006. Presented in Raleigh, NC.

Republished with permission of the International Institute for Sustainable Development (IISD) www.iisd.org.

Endnotes

Abbreviations for frequently used terms:

CARB California Air Resources Board
DoA   Department of Agriculture
DoE   Department of Energy
EIA   Energy Information Administration, DoE
EPA   Environmental Protection Agency
ERS   Economic Research Service, DoA
NASS National Agricultural Statistical Service, DoA

PART I
Chapter 2

1. The White House, "The President's Program for the United States Energy Security: The Energy Security Corporation," August 1979, pp. 29, 33, 40.

2. Inflation as measured by the GDP deflator, "Economic Report of the President: 2008 Report," Spreadsheet Table B-3.

3. DoE, *DOE News*, "Energy Secretary Presents National Energy Policy," July 17, 1981, p. 1.

4. Reagan Public Archives/Speeches, 1982, "Question and Answer Session with Farmers in State Center, Iowa, August 2, 1982," p.3.

5. Doug Koplow, "Overview of Liquid Biofuels Industry in the United States," EarthTrack, Inc., October 2006, p. 17, available at www.earthlink.net.

6. EIA, online data from Alternative Fueled Vehicles, Vehicles in Use, Table V1, Footnote c, available at www.eia.doe.gov/cneaf/alternate/page/atftables/afvtrans_v1.xls.

7. See National Ethanol Vehicle Coalition, data for June 8, 2008, as reported online in "E85 Refueling Stations by State," available at http://www.e85refueling.com/states.php?PHPSESSID=e6c99 cc391807f3a9b6a4ce41b912f84.

8. James Bovard, "Archer Daniels Midland: A Case Study in Corporate Welfare," CATO Institute, Policy Analysis no. 241, September 26, 1995, pp. 8–10.

9. EIA, Ethanol Energy Timeline, 1980-85, available at www.EIA. DOE.gov.

10. The White House, "Fact Sheet," The President's Alcohol Fuels Program, January 11, 1980, p. 3.

11. DoE, *DOE News*, "Energy Secretary Presents National Energy Policy," July 17, 1981, p. 5.

12. Milton R. Copulos, "Reagan's Fading Energy Agenda," "Backgrounder #204," Heritage Foundation, August 17, 1982.

13. Reagan Public Archives, "Presidential Announcement of Proposed Legislation to Reduce Funding for the National Synthetic Fuels Program," May 14, 1984.

14. *President's Budget Appendix*, Fiscal Year 1983, pp. I-F50, I-R16.

15. Doug Koplow, "Biofuels—At What Cost? Government Support for Ethanol and Biodiesel in the U.S.: Earth Track, Inc., October 2006, p. 17, available at www.globalsubsidies.org. Prepared for Global Subsidies Initiative, International Institute for Sustainable Development.

16. John A. Herrick, "Federal Project Financing Incentives for Green Industries: Renewable Energy and Beyond," *Natural Resources Journal*, Winter 2003, p. 81.

17. DoA/Agricultural Statistics Board/National Agricultural Statistics Service (NASS), "Grain Stocks Historical Track Records," April 2007, p. 6.

18. DoA/NASS, "U.S. & All States Data-Corn Field," accessible by online query at www.nass.usda.gov/QuickStats/index2.jsp.

19. Michael J. Weiss, "The High Octane Ethanol Lobby," the *New York Times*, April 1, 1990.

20. See comments received for National Highway Traffic Safety Administration's Final Rule, Automotive Fuel Economy Manufacturing Incentives for Alternative Fuel Vehicles, October 1, 2004, available at www.nhtsa.dot.gov/cars/rules/CAFE/Rulemaking/AMFAFinalRule2004.htm.

21. Pres. Ronald Reagan, Remarks on Signing the Alternative Motor Fuels Act of 1988, Reagan Presidential Library Archives, October 14, 1988.

22. A 1990 budget agreement between the President and Congressional Democrats provided for a $500 billion reduction in the budget deficit over five years.

23. DoE, *National Energy Strategy*, First Edition, 1991/2, p. 2, February 1991.

24. Ibid., passim.

25. Ibid., p. 6.

26. Ibid., p. 4.

27. Ibid., p. 16.

28. Renewable Fuels Association, Industry Statistics, Ethanol Industry Overview, available at www.ethanolrfa.org/industry/statistics/#EIO.

29. Congressional Research Service (CRS), "Ethanol and Clean Air: The 'Reg-Neg' Controversy and Subsequent Events," CRS Report for Congress, June 22, 1993, and Edward P. Weber, *Pluralism by the Rules: Conflict and Cooperation in Environmental Regulation*, (Washington, D.C.: Georgetown University Press, 1998).

30. Environmental Protection Agency, "Drinking Water Advisory: Consumer Acceptability Advice and Health Effects Analysis of Methyl Tertiary Butyl Ether (MTBE)," EPA Fact Sheet, December 1997.

31. *Federal Register*, 58 FR 68343, December 27, 1993.

32. See *American Petroleum Institute v. Environmental Protection Agency*, U.S. Court of Appeals for the District of Columbia, 1995. A discussion of the "Reg Neg" process appears in Ellen

Siegler, "Regulatory Negotiations and Other Rulemaking Processes: Strengths and Weaknesses from an Industry View," *Duke Law Journal*, 46 1429 (April 1997).

33. "Fuel's Gold: ADM Million-Dollar Soft Money Donations Help the Ethanol Tax Break Survive, According to Common Cause Survey," June 1998, *The Washington Post*, available at www.washingtonpost.com/wp-srv/politics/campaigns/keyraces98/stories/keycash061198.htm.

34. National Energy Policy Development Group (chaired by Vice Pres. Dick Cheney), "National Energy Policy Report," May 2001.

35. The White House, "The President's Energy Legislative Agenda," June 2001.

36. Energy and Environment Study Institute, "Status Report: 2002 Farm Bill Energy Title (H.R.2646)," August 2003, available at www.eesi.org/publications/Energy%20Title%20Update_%20 8_03.PDF.

37. "Regulation of Fuels and Fuel Additives: Renewable Fuel Standard Program," Federal Register: May 1, 2007 (Volume 72, Number 83), pp. 23899-23948.

38. Executive Office of the President/Office of Management and Budget, "Statement of Administration Policy," H.R. 6 H. R., Energy Policy Act of 2005; April 20, 2005; p. 1.

39. President's State of the Union address, section on the Advanced Energy Initiative," January 31, 2006; p. 1.

40. President's State of the Union address, section "Twenty in Ten: Strengthening America's Energy Security," January 23, 2007; p. 1.

41. Burton C. English, Daniel G. De La Torre Ugarte, et al, "25% Renewable Energy for the United States By 2025: Agricultural and Economic Impacts," University of Tennessee, November 2006; and "Biomass as Feedstock for a Bioenergy and Bioproducts Industry: The Technical Feasibility of a Billion-Ton Annual Supply," DoE/DoA, April 2005.

42. *Ethanol Producer*, "A Billion Ton Forecast," July 2007.

43. America's Energy Futures, "New U. Tenn. Report Outlines Renewable Energy Roadmap," Press Release; November 15,

2006, accessible at www.25x25.org/index.php?option=com_content&task=view&id=156&Itemid=56 .

44. EIA, www.eia.doe.gov/oiaf/servicerpt/mtbeban/; CRS, www.ncseonline.org/NLE/CRSreports/air/air-26.cfm.

45. DoA, "USDA 2007 Farm Bill Proposals, Title IX: Energy," available at www.usda.gov/documents/fbenergy_07.doc.

46. *Wall Street Journal*, "An Ethanol Bailout?" December 24, 2009.

PART II
Chapter 3

1. Renewable Fuels Association, "One Year Anniversary of Energy Legislation Highlighting Success of Renewable Fuels Standard" and American Coalition for Ethanol, "What is ethanol?" January 26, 2009.

2. EIA, "Energy and Economic Impacts of Implementing Both a 25-Percent Renewables Portfolio Standard and a 25-Percent Renewable Fuels Standard by 2025," Reference Case, Table 11, September 2007, accessible at http://www.eia.doe.gov/oiaf/servicerpt/eeim/pdf/table11.pdf.

3. EIA, *Monthly Energy Review*, November 2008, Table 10.3—Fuel Ethanol Overview.

4. There is a basic difference between a "tight" oil market, where prices are increasing sharply because of a market imbalance between supply and demand, and an oil market in which one or more suppliers encounter a severe, extended interruption to their operations. Severe interruptions, such as the Persian Gulf War imposed in 1990–91 and the Iranian Revolution in 1978–79, can occur in either tight or slack oil markets.

5. DoE/EIA, *Annual Energy Outlook 2008*, June 2008.

6. Bill O'Grady, Chief Investment Strategist, Wachovia Securities, "Weekly Geopolitical Report: Iranian Showdown," July 7, 2008, p. 3.

7. Ibid.

8. Interagency Working Group, "Strategic Petroleum Reserve: Analysis of Size Options," February 1990, Table IV (prepared by the Central Intelligence Agency).

9. DoE/Fossil Energy, "Fact Sheet on IEA Member Country Oil Stocks and Emergency Response Potential," undated, accessible at http://fossil.energy.gov/programs/reserves/spr/IEA_factsheet _9-05.pdf.

10. Ibid.

11. DoA/National Agricultural Statistics Service (NASS), "Crop Production Historical Track Records," April 2009, accessible at http://usda.mannlib.cornell.edu/usda/current/htrcp/htrcp-04-30-2009.pdf.

12. DoA/NASS, "U.S. & All States Data-Corn field," accessible by online query at www.nass.usda.gov/QuickStats/index2.jsp. In addition to national crop statistics, see weekly data on state growing conditions; for example, the statistics provided in DoA, National Agricultural Statistics Service, "Weekly Weather Crop Bulletin State Stories," April 15, 2008, detailing problems in the Midwest states in spring 2008, accessible at http://usda.mannlib .cornell.edu/usda/current/htrcp/htrcp-04-30-2009.pdf .

13. George Lobsenz, "Amid Soaring Gasoline Prices, U.S. Ethanol Producers Cutting Back," *The Energy Daily*, June 26, 2008.

14. "Strategic Petroleum Reserve," Table IV.

Chapter 4

15. Michael Wang, May Wu, and Hong Huo, "Life-cycle energy and greenhouse gas emission impacts of different corn ethanol plant types," *Environmental Research Letters*, 2, May 22, 2007.

16. EPA, "E85 and Flex Fuel Vehicles," January 30, 2009, p. 2, accessible at www.epa.gov/otaq/smartway/growandgo/documents/factsheet-e85.htm.

17. Secretary of Energy Samuel Bodman, testimony before the House Committee on Energy and Commerce, February 8, 2007, p. 1.

18. DoE/Energy Efficiency and Renewable Energy, "The complete ethanol life cycle picture", January 28, 2009, accessible at http://www1.eere.energy.gov/vehiclesandfuels/pdfs/program/ethanol_brochure_bw.pdf.

19. "E85 and Flex Fuel Vehicles," p. 2.

20. M. Wang, C, Saricks, and D. Santini, "Effects of Fuel Ethanol Use on Fuel-Cycle Energy and Greenhouse Gas Emissions," Argonne National Laboratory, Transportation Technology R&D Center technical report, January 1999, p. 1.

21. "Life-cycle energy"

22. Ibid.

23. DoA/ERS, online Data Sets, Fertilizer Use and Prices, Table 10, "Nitrogen used on corn, rate per fertilized acre receiving nitrogen, selected states," updated November 20, 2008, accessible at www .ers.usda.gov/DATA/FERTILIZERUSEtables/table10.xls.

24. Roman Keeney and Thomas W. Hertel, Global Trade Analysis Project, "The Indirect Land Use Impacts of U.S. Biofuels Policies: The Importance of Acreage Yield and Bilateral Trade Responses," GTAP Working Paper No. 52, October 22, 2008.

25. "Life-cycle energy"

26. RSC Advancing the Chemical Sciences, "Biofuels could boost global warming, finds study," September 21, 2007, accessible at http://www.rsc.org/chemistryworld/News/2007/September/21090701.asp.

27. UVa Today, "Tyler Environmental Prize Goes to University of Virginia's James Galloway, Author of Key Papers on Nitrogen Cascade's Ecological Effects," March 27, 2008.

28. Timothy Searchinger, et al., "Use of U.S. Croplands for Biofuels Increases Greenhouse Gases Through Emissions from Land-Use Change," Science Express Report, February 7, 2008, p. 1.

29. Ibid.

30. Joe Fargione et al., "Land clearing and the biofuel carbon debt." Science, February 29, 2008.

31. "The Indirect Land Use Impacts"

32. M. Wang and Z. Hua, letter to Science, March 14, 2008.

33. Alex Ferrell and Michael O'Hare, Energy & Resources Group, University of California/Berkeley, "GHG emissions from indirect land use change," memorandum to John Courtis of the CARB,

January 12, 2008.

34. EPA, Notice of Proposed Rule Making, "Regulation of Fuels and Fuel Additives: Renewable Fuels Standard Program," May 5, 2009, page 317, accessible at http://www.scribd.com/doc/14983581/EPA-Renewable-Fuel-Standard-Program-Notice-of-Proposed-Rule-Making.

35. Ibid, page 193.

36. Ibid, page 299.

37. Ibid, page 315.

38. EIA, Annual Energy Outlook 2009, March 2009, accessible at http://www.eia.doe.gov/oiaf/aeo/supplement/index.html.

39. Coordinating Research Council (CRC), "Effects of Ethanol and Volatility Parameters on Exhaust Emissions," CRC Project No. E-67, January 30, 2006.

40. CRC, "Fuel Permeation from Automotive Systems: E0, E6, E10, E20 and E85," CRC Report No. E-65-3, December 2006.

41. CARB, "Initial Statement Of Reasons, Proposed Amendments to California Phase 3 Gasoline Regulations," Staff Report, April 27, 2007.

42. CARB, Final Regulation Order, "2007 Amendments to the California Phase 3 Reformulated Gasoline Regulations," issued August 29, 2008.

43. M. Z. Jacobson, "Effects of Ethanol (E85) versus Gasoline Vehicles on Cancer and Mortality in the United States," *Environmental Science and Technology*, vol. 41, no. 11, 2007.

44. DoE, "Energy Demands on Water Resources, Report to Congress on the Interdependency of Energy and Water," December 2006.

45. AGLW Water Management Group, "Crop Water Management—Maize," United Nations Food and Agriculture Organization, accessible at www.fao.org/landandwater/aglw/cropwater/maize.stm.

46. Shiney Varghese, "Biofuels and Global Water Challenges," Institute for Agriculture and Trade Policy, October 2007, accessible at http://www.iatp.org/iatp/publications.cfm?accountID=451&refID=100547.

47. A.K. Chapagain, and A.Y. Hoekstra, "The global component of freshwater demand and supply: an assessment of virtual water flows between nations as a result of trade in agricultural and industrial products," *Water International*, V. 33, No. 1, March 2008, pp.19-32.

48. Ethanol Producer, "More Corn a Cause for Concern," January 2008," accessible at www.ethanolproducer.com/article.jsp?article _id=3569.

49. "Energy Demands on Water Resources"

50. National Research Council of the National Academies, "Water Implications of Biofuels Production in the United States," Report in Brief, October 2007.

51. "More Corn a Cause for Concern"

Chapter 5

52. DoA/DoE, "Report to Congress on the Feasibility of Including Biomass Fuels as Part of the Strategic Petroleum Reserve," April 2002.

53. "The Impact of Ethanol Use on Food Prices and Greenhouse-Gas Emissions," Congressional Budget Office, CBO Paper, April 2009.

Chapter 6

54. Internal Revenue Service, "Fiscal Year 2008 Enforcement Results," Total Individual Returns, p. 2, accessible at http://www .irs.gov/pub/irs-news/2008_enforcement.pdf.

55. *Annual Energy Outlook 2009*, Table 58 (Light-Duty Vehicle Stock by Technology Type).

56. Bureau of Census, National and State Population Estimates, accessible at http://www.census.gov/popest/states/NST-ann-est.html.

57. DoE, "Fact Sheet: Gas Prices and Oil Consumption Would Increase Without Biofuels," June 11, 2008, p. 1.

58. EIA, "Energy and Economic Impacts of Implementing Both a 25-Percent RPS and a 25-Percent RFS by 2025," reference case, September 2007, accessible at http://www.eia.doe.gov/oiaf/

servicerpt/eeim/policy.html. The analysis used a reference-case assumption of a U.S. competitive market policy.

59. See the Energy Security section of this book for EIA estimates of ethanol consumption under a competitive market-ethanol policy.

60. See "Ethanol is a Budget Buster: Increased Mandate and Subsidies Would Raise Food Prices and Strain Federal Budget," by William Yeatman, Competitive Enterprise Institute, *CEI On Point* article, July 31, 2007 (http://cei.org/studies-point/ethanol-budget-buster) for which I provided much of the budget information; this chapter substantially expands and enhances the discussion of the costs raised in the Yeatman article.

61. *The Washington Post*, "Product Recalls," Lexus Vehicles section, January 17, 2009, p. D1.

62. DoA in collaboration with DoE, "Report to Congress on the Feasibility of Including Biomass Fuels as Part of the Strategic Petroleum Reserve," April 2002.

63. PR Newswire, "Exxon, Chevron Face Ethanol Class Action by Kabateck Brown Kellner, LLP," April 7, 2008.

64. See Environmental Working Group website, http://www.ewg.org/farmsubsidies.

65. To identify the likely increase in net income for corn and soybean farmers attributable to federal intervention (mainly the Renewable Fuels Standard, or RFS), estimates of post-RFS net income average were subtracted from pre-RFS income for each of the Midwestern states. The average of net incomes across the period from 2000 to 2003 was selected as a representative, pre-RFS baseline. Similarly, the immediate post-RFS era was represented with the averages for incomes in 2004 to 2007. Since net income at the state level is for all agricultural activities—including all crops produced and sold, as well as livestock—that amount was adjusted downward based on the portion of total agricultural sales accounted for by corn and soybeans together. (No net-income information is available for farms that grow only, or largely, corn and soybeans.) The author believes that the

resulting estimate of the immediate increase in net incomes will understate the ultimate increase over the period 2008 to 2017, since rising RFS targets in future years are likely to result in further increases in corn and soybean demand.

66. To identify the likely per-acre increase in farmland values attributable to government intervention (mainly the Renewable Fuels Standard, or RFS), state estimates of the land value for 2008 (as a proxy for post-RFS) were subtracted from those for 2004 (as a proxy for pre-RFS). That per-acre amount was then multiplied by the number of acres reported by the NASS for 2008 for the corn and soybeans harvested within each state. That procedure yields a conservative estimate of full impact, since the per-acre values are likely to rise considerably as the RFS quantities increase through 2015. For example, in many of the Midwestern states, corn and soybean farms occupy highly valued land. As a result, using the state average probably understates the increase in value.

67. "Energy and Economic Impacts"

Chapter 7

68. "The Impact of Ethanol Use on Food Prices"

69. *The Washington Post*, "Woman is Killed When Railroad Cars Explode," June 21, 2009, p. A6.

About the Author

....

Ken G. Glozer received his post-graduate public policy education from 1970–1997 while working for the White House Office of Management & Budget. He was a charter member of the career Senior Executive Service. He has served as a SES member for nearly twenty years, first heading up the energy and agriculture budget examining division, and then a policy studies division. He has worked on and played a key staff role in the formulation of every Presidential National Energy Plan, beginning with the Nixon Administration's Project Independence, the Carter Administration's Nation Energy Plans I, II, the market reliance strategy/policies of the Reagan years, the National Energy Strategy for Bush I. He also worked on farm bills from 1975 through 1992, the Clean Air Act Amendments of 1990, and countless other federal energy, environment, agricultural, and natural resource policies and programs.

From 1993–1996, while at OMB, he was detailed to the Department of Energy and worked on the $7 billion per year environmental cleanup of all former nuclear weapons production facilities throughout the U.S.

Since leaving the OMB, he was employed by ICF International Inc., a private consulting firm, specializing in energy and environment policies and programs.

From 1999 through the present, he is employed as the President of OMB Professionals, Inc., a Washington D.C. based private firm that specializes in serving private companies, trade associations and nonprofit interest groups on a range of federal policies, programs, and issues. He is also an expert on federal agency lending programs and practices.

Mr. Glozer has a BS from West Virginia University, a MBA from George Washington University, and a MBA Upgrade from Syracuse University. He can be contacted at: KGlozer@ombpros.com.

Energy Policy

The Hoover Institution's Shultz-Stephenson Task Force on Energy Policy addresses energy policy in the United States and its effects on our domestic and international political priorities, particularly our national security.

As a result of volatile and rising energy prices and increasing global concern about climate change, two related and compelling issues—threats to national security and adverse effects of energy usage on global climate—have emerged as key adjuncts to America's energy policy; the task force will explore these subjects in detail. The task force's goals are to gather comprehensive information on current scientific and technological developments, survey the contingent policy actions, and offer a range of prescriptive policies to address our varied energy challenges. The task force will focus on public policy at all levels, from individual to global. It will then recommend policy initiatives, large and small, that can be undertaken to the advantage of both private enterprises and governments acting individually and in concert.

Index

administration, 16, 22–23; in Clinton administration, 46; on greenhouse gas emission requirements, 90–91; in Reagan administration, 24, 26–27
Lugar, Richard G., 26

McClure, James, 28
methyl tertiary butyl ether. *See* MTBE
Mexico, oil imports from, 78f, 81
Midwestern states: benefits of corn ethanol policies for, 145–51, 158; corn production in, 6, 23, 133–41. *See also* corn production; distribution of ethanol from, 87; employment in, 129–30; ethanol market in, 6, 7, 17, 18, 26, 35, 38, 53; farm income in, 147, 148f, 150f, 206n65; land values in, 147–51, 150f, 207n66; MTBE ban in, 64; political representatives of, 26, 48, 59–60; soybean farms in, 133–41; subsidy payments to farmers in, 137f, 145–46, 146f; weather conditions in, 76, 83, 85. *See also* weather conditions
mileage per gallon, ethanol affecting, 141, 142–44
Minnesota, corn, soybean, and ethanol production in, 140f; estimated total federal benefits for, 150f, 152f; farm income in, 148f; number of farms in, 137f, 152f; per farm average benefits

for, 152f; subsidy payments for, 137f, 146f
Mississippi River, nitrogen runoff in, 122
Missouri, corn, soybean, and ethanol production in, 140f; farm income in, 148f; number of farms in, 137f, 152f; per farm average benefits for, 152f; subsidy payments for, 137f, 146f
MTBE (methyl tertiary butyl ether), 36, 38, 43, 50, 51; federal ban on, 51, 65; liability lawsuits associated with, 58, 64, 65; octane rating of gasoline with, 7, 38, 46; state bans on, 7, 10, 64; water contamination from, 46, 51, 64

National Agricultural Statistics Service (NASS), 83
National Alcohol Fuels Commission, 16
National Corn Growers Association, 4, 22, 26, 50
National Energy Act of 1978, 15, 16
National Energy Plans of Carter administration, 15–16, 18, 20
National Energy Policy Development Group in Bush II administration, 49, 52–53, 55
National Energy Strategy in Bush I administration, 34, 36, 38–41
National Ethanol Vehicle Coalition, 35, 50